For Susan,
Love

BROTHERS ALL

A Play in Three Acts

by

Howard Rubenstein

based on
Fyodor Dostoyevsky's novel
The Brothers Karamazov
as translated by Constance Garnett

GRANITE HILLS PRESS™

BROTHERS ALL
A Play in Three Acts
by Howard Rubenstein
based on Fyodor Dostoyevsky's novel
The Brothers Karamazov
as translated by Constance Garnett

Published 2007 by Granite Hills Press™
SAN 298-072X

Cover by Chuck Conners

Publisher's Cataloging-in-Publication
Rubenstein, Howard S., 1931-
   Brothers all : a play in three acts / by Howard Rubenstein ; based on Fyodor Dostoyevsky's novel The brothers Karamazov / as translated by Constance Garnett.
   p. cm.
   LCCN 2006938252
   ISBN-13: 978-1-929468-11-9
   ISBN-10: 1-929468-11-3

   1. Fathers and sons--Drama. 2. Brothers--Drama.
   I. Dostoyevsky, Fyodor, 1821-1881. Bratia Karamazovy.
   II. Title.

PS3618.U3167B76 2007   812'.6
                      QBI06-600634

Printed in the United States of America

To all who respect humanity in its diversity

ACKNOWLEDGMENTS

I thank all those who helped realize the script, the premiere, and the book of *Brothers All*. The play was first produced at 6th@Penn Theatre, San Diego, on February 19, 2006.

It is a pleasure to acknowledge the premiere's crew and cast: Barry Bosworth, Director/actor (Karleton); Bobbi Bosworth, Stage Manager; and cast (in alphabetical order): Terence J. Burke (Cardinal/Prosecutor), Hal Conley (Gregory), Jude Evans (Alex), Chris Hastings (Father Jeremiah/Defender), Laura Ingram (Theresa), Jesse Keller (Ian), Tony Misiano (Melvin), Jude Morgan (Mrs. Holiday/Martha), Donal Pugh (Dr. Hart/Police Captain), Stephen Rowe (Father Ignatius/Judge), Ryan Schulze (Visiting Priest/Visitor/Guard/Foreman), Andrea Tobar (Kathryn), and Jonathan Wilcox (Douglas).

I also thank the director and cast for asking the questions that led to a clarified script. I thank Ingar Quist for editing the final draft of the book. And I give special thanks to Judith S. Rubenstein for her love, support, and encouragement not only as my wife but also as editor, critic, and co-producer.

Howard Rubenstein
San Diego
December 10, 2006

INTRODUCTION

The play *Brothers All* is based on Fyodor Dostoyevsky's novel *The Brothers Karamazov* (as translated by Constance Garnett), but it is not a dramatization of it. The novel has many subplots and characters, but the play does not. The novel is constructed almost like a cubist painting: It is broken into parts that do not always fit, are sometimes missing, or seem to belong to another painting. The play is less complex. It restricts itself mostly to the main plot and the principal characters.

The novel deals with many psychological, medical, sociological, religious, and political issues, some of which are as universal and relevant today as when Dostoyevsky wrote about them. The ones I considered most significant I incorporated into the play.

Thirty years before the novel was written, Dostoyevsky was condemned to death for expressing his ideas on many of those issues, because they were considered dangerously socialistic. At the last minute, the czar commuted the sentence from death to four years of imprisonment in Siberia. When similar ideas reappeared in *The Brothers Karamazov*, they were condemned again, not by a devout and czarist society but by the novel's devout and czarist narrator. Had Dostoyevsky undergone a born-again nationalistic and religious conversion sometime during those thirty years, or was the narrator a ploy to prevent another death sentence?

The novel reveals with astonishing clarity religion's inadequacy in explaining the suffering of children; the difference between the teachings of the founder of a religion and the dogma of the institution that claims to be the sole repository and interpreter of those teachings; a religion's misguided belief that it alone possesses the truth and therefore all humanity needs to believe in what that religion dictates; and the immeasurable misery that such a belief, however sincere, inflicts on humanity. The novel brilliantly reveals the absence of safeguards against the miscarriage of justice in cases in which one individual is assumed to bear all responsibility for a crime. And the novel extolls, as did Schiller and Beethoven, a redemption that comes about not only through suffering but also through joy. All those issues and ideas I incorporated into my play.

Dostoyevsky is not considered a comic writer, but the novel is punctuated with humor, which may have been overlooked because much of it is irreverent and Dostoyevsky veiled it. In writing the play, I removed the veil. Some critics were indignant, believing the humor was not only outrageous but also original with me.

In addition to the issues and ideas just discussed, the novel contains many outdated, unsupported, and even hateful notions. Although they are still very much alive in some circles, I had no intention of perpetuating them in my play. They include the notion that epilepsy is a sign of insanity and a cause of malicious behavior; that czarist Russia, along with its institutions, is the model for an ideal society; that Jews (with the possible exception of the musicians) and Muslims (without exception) personify evil; and that deception, rejection, and torment are characteristic of the male-female relationship.

Because it was my intent that the play deal with universal issues and ideas, I removed the story from Russia in the nineteenth century and placed it in a time "not long ago" and a place "not far away."

Howard Rubenstein

BROTHERS ALL

CHARACTERS

(in order of importance, more or less)

KARLETON. A very rich man, middle-aged. Father of Douglas, Ian, Alex, and Melvin.

DOUGLAS (DOUG). Karleton's eldest son, an army lieutenant, age twenty-eight. Half brother to Ian and Alex. (His mother was Karleton's first wife, who died when Doug was a child.)

IAN. Karleton's second son, a writer, age twenty-four. Half brother to Douglas; full brother to Alex. (His mother was Karleton's second wife, who abandoned Karleton and their children.)

ALEX. Karleton's youngest son, a seminary student, age twenty. Half brother to Douglas; full brother to Ian. (His mother was Karleton's second wife.)

MELVIN. Karleton's illegitimate son, Karleton's cook, age twenty-four. Half brother to Douglas, Ian, and Alex. (His mother was a homeless single woman, who died giving birth to him.)

GREGORY. Karleton's servant, middle-aged.

MARTHA. Gregory's wife and Karleton's housekeeper, middle-aged.

FATHER JEREMIAH. Corpulent, indulgent, middle-aged.

FATHER IGNATIUS. Lean, ascetic, middle-aged.

VISITING PRIEST. In his twenties.

MRS. HOLIDAY. A wealthy divorcée, middle-aged.

THERESA. A waitress, in her early twenties, attractive, flirtatious.

KATHRYN. An heiress, in her early twenties, attractive, reserved, Doug's former fiancée.

DR. HART. Family doctor, middle-aged.

PROSECUTOR.

DEFENDER.

JUDGE.

POLICE CAPTAIN.

CARDINAL. The Grand Inquisitor, a character in Ian's play.

STRANGER. A Christlike figure, in his thirties, a character in Ian's play.

VISITOR. A devilish figure, resembling Ian.

GUARD.

FOREMAN OF THE JURY.

SCENES

TIME: Not long ago
PLACE: Not far away

Because of the many scenes, the sets should be minimal so that scene changes proceed swiftly, in most cases within thirty seconds.

Brothers All

ACT I

SCENE 1

On the street. DOUGLAS and KATHRYN are standing facing each other. He kisses her softly. She exits. THERESA enters. DOUGLAS and THERESA kiss passionately. He exits. KARLETON enters, approaches THERESA, puts his arm around her waist, draws her close, trying to kiss her, but she squirms out of his arms, steps away, turns, smiles, and coquettishly blows him a kiss. She exits. He smiles, shrugs his shoulders, and exits.

(Fade-out.)

SCENE 2

Reception room of the rectory. It is almost 1:00 p.m., and the room is flooded with reflected sunlight. A beautifully framed large reproduction of a Renaissance Madonna and Child is displayed prominently. A small table holds a pair of silver candlesticks and a decanter of ruby port. KARLETON and IAN are seated and momentarily silent.

KARLETON. Did you see the fancy tombstones in the cemetery? The dead buried there have already paid their way to heaven.

IAN. Dad!

KARLETON. Sorry! I promised to behave.

IAN. I wonder what's keeping Doug.

KARLETON. (*Staring attentively at the picture of the Madonna and Child, then walking slowly and gazing about the room.*) Oh, the Devil take all this! A show built up over centuries with nothing but charlatanism and nonsense! (*Returning to the picture of the Madonna and pretending to speak to her.*) We're here, Madame! The least you can do is offer us a glass of wine! (*Genuflecting, making the sign of the cross.*)

IAN. Dad, what are you doing?

KARLETON. When in Rome, do as the Romans! Did you know that the men here look at one another but not at a single woman? And they're hoping to live like that through eternity! That's truly amazing!

IAN. Dad, please be quiet!

KARLETON. Do you know there's a Greek monastery on Mount Athos where no women are allowed, and there are no creatures of the female sex—no cows, no ewes, no hens?

IAN. Dad, please! You can't go on talking like this!

Soon Father Jeremiah will be here; and if you continue to say things like this, you're bound to say them inadvertently in his presence.

KARLETON. You're right! I'll be good. But I can't imagine why you're so touchy. Are you afraid the good father will talk to me about my sins—or yours? Do you have any sins, Ian? Everybody does. What are yours? I've yet to discover them. But don't worry about my behavior. I'll be good.

(*A carillon plays and strikes the hour of one.*)

Well, it's one o'clock.

(FR. JEREMIAH *and* ALEX *enter.*)

Look at that! Right on time! Everyone but my son Douglas!

FR. JEREMIAH. (*Cheerfully, hand extended to* KARLETON.) Hello, Mr. Karleton!

(*They shake hands.*)

Delighted to meet you!

KARLETON. I'm sure you've heard *so* much about me.

FR. JEREMIAH. As a matter of fact, I have.

KARLETON. In spite of all you've heard, Father, I do believe in God, I really do, even though, I must confess, I've been having some doubts lately.

FR. JEREMIAH. (*Sits.*) Please, everyone sit down.

(*They sit.*)

KARLETON. (*To* FR. JEREMIAH.) Father, tell me the truth. Do I annoy you by the things I say?

FR. JEREMIAH. My son, don't be troubled by such thoughts. Be comfortable! Make yourself at home!

KARLETON. Father, you must never invite me to be at home. Don't risk it! (*Suddenly falling to his knees before* FR. JEREMIAH.) "Blessed be the womb that bore you and the teats that gave you suck!" That's Luke 11:27. (*Looking at* IAN *and* ALEX.) My family marvels when I quote Scripture. (*To* FR. JEREMIAH.) O Father of truth, I am a liar and a father of lies! But tell me, is it true, the story about the holy martyr who, after his head was cut off, stood up, (*Pantomiming.*) picked up his head, then tenderly kissed it? Is that a true story?

FR. JEREMIAH. No, it's not true.

KARLETON. Still, I didn't make it up. After I heard that story, my faith was shaken. (*Sitting.*) Father, do you think I always play the fool? I've been putting you to the test to see whether you could bear me. You have passed the test. "Teacher, what must I do to gain eternal life?" (*Standing.*) That's Matthew 19:16.

> (*Suddenly the door from the outside opens, and* DOUG *rushes in, sheepish and flustered.*)

DOUG. I hope you'll forgive me for having kept you waiting, but Melvin—my father told Melvin to tell me about the appointment, and Melvin told me it was at two o'clock. Thank God that Gregory called me a few minutes ago to remind me the appointment was at one.

> (FR. JEREMIAH *stands and shakes* DOUG*'s hand.*)

FR. JEREMIAH. Don't be upset, my son. There was a

misunderstanding, that's all. It's of no consequence. (*Pause.*) Now that we're all here, shall we begin? We have gathered for a purpose. Mr. Karleton, you and your son Douglas have been engaged in a dispute, but you did not want to consult attorneys. You decided, on the advice of Alex here, to consult me.

KARLETON. (*Jumping to his feet.*) Father, this son of mine has the nerve to arrive late and blame it on others!

DOUG. Father Jeremiah, you took the trouble to arrange this meeting, and all my father wants to do is make a scene!

KARLETON.   First he blames Melvin, and now he blames me! He accuses me of being a miser. He says I have hidden his money throughout my house—in my dresser, under the mattress, in my shoes, in my socks—everywhere but in his pocket! He says I've cheated him out of his rightful inheritance, gifts from his mother!

DOUG. Well, it's true, isn't it?

KARLETON. (*Changing the subject.*) Father, would you believe that the most wonderful young woman has fallen in love with him, a girl from a good family, but now he's taken up with a tramp who sleeps with everyone and on whom he's already squandered a fortune. The whole town is talking about his life of debauchery. Some behavior for an army officer!

DOUG. Shut up! That you above all should speak a word against her is an outrage, you old hypocrite!

KARLETON. See how a son speaks to a father!

DOUG. I was hoping to get my father's blessing on my marriage to the woman I love. And what do I find? A depraved and despicable clown!

KARLETON. You have abandoned your fiancée for another woman!

DOUG. Yes!   Because I happen to love her! And

apparently so do you! I wish you were dead!

KARLETON. Ah! Now he wishes me dead! Maybe he intends to kill me! Forgive me, all of you, but I must go! (*Rushing from the room and slamming the door.*)

ALEX. We must apologize, Your Reverence, for our father's behavior. But I know that he's regretting what he said and that he'll soon convey his apologies to you.

(*The door flies open.*)

KARLETON. (*Laughing, from the doorway.*) Quite a vanishing act, wouldn't you say? Well, I could tell that you missed me, and so I've returned! Actually, I thought there's no hope of my ever changing my ways, so I may as well return and embarrass you for all I'm worth. (*Pause.*) Well, Father, are you going to invite me to come back in or not?

FR. JEREMIAH. Forgive me, Mr. Karleton! Come in! Gentlemen, I beg you to set aside your differences and be united in love and family harmony.

KARLETON. Stock phrases delivered most sancti-moniously! I know them all by heart! I don't like lying, Father. I want the truth! (*Gazing about the room.*) But the truth is not to be found here! (*Drawing close to the table with the candlesticks and port. Holding up and inspecting a candlestick.*) Well, what's this? Old port wine and shining silver! My, my, Father, who has provided this? (*Setting down the candlestick.*) Who has paid for it? The poor, that's who! You bleed them.

Well, I'm going. (*Walking toward the door.*) And when I leave this time, I won't return. I'm taking revenge for all the humiliation I endured as a youth. This church has indeed played an important role in my life!

FR. JEREMIAH.   Jesus said, "Do good to those who hate
    you."
KARLETON.   And so forth and so on and the rest of your
    rigmarole! I go, Father! (*Exits, slamming the door.*)

    (*After an instant, the door reopens.*)

Forgive me. I forgot to say good-bye. (*Sugary.*)   Good-
    bye. (*He mockingly blows a kiss and gently closes the
    door.*)

    (*Fade-out.*)

                        SCENE 3

*Karleton's garden, that afternoon. DOUG is sitting on
the garden bench, drinking beer and humming Beethoven's
music to Schiller's "Ode to Joy." After a moment ALEX
enters. DOUG stands. They embrace.*

ALEX.   Doug, you seem a bit—excited.
DOUG.   Ah! You were going to say "drunk." Don't
    worry. I'm not drunk, just a little high.

    (*They sit.*)

    You know, I've fallen in love. But, Alex, they don't
    teach about love in theology school. They speak of it
    all right, but they don't teach it.   Do you know, a
    man will fall in love with a beauty, with a woman's
    face or body, and he'll abandon everything for her—
    wife and children—why, he'd sell his own mother and
    father, even his own country, if he could.   (*Gazing
    upward, smiling.*) Look at that sky, how blue! How

green this garden! How beautiful the light through the leaves! (*To* ALEX.) What brings you here?

ALEX. I've come to see Dad. Why are you here?

DOUG. I've come to see him, too, to tell him my plans. I'm resigning from the army. My discharge should be coming through soon.

ALEX. I thought you loved the army.

DOUG. (*Pacing now and through most of the scene.*) The army was all right. It was combat I hated. Once, at the height of a battle, I was driving a truck through snow and sleet in a war-torn village. Half the homes were bombed and burning. As I drove, I saw row upon row of women, all thin and wan. There was one in particular, tall and bony, holding a crying baby, its fists blue from the cold. I wanted to stop the truck. I wanted to end the war. I wanted to end all wars forever, in spite of the impossibility, with all the recklessness that Father and I are famous for. I wanted the whole world to sing songs of joy.

ALEX. That's a noble thought. You have nothing to be ashamed of.

DOUG. Ever since I've been home, I've been wondering what happened to that baby with the blue fists. Whom did that child ever harm? How many children's deaths am I responsible for, children who harmed no one? Sometimes I think I deserve to die for all those children's deaths.

ALEX. People getting killed in war isn't your fault.

DOUG. Now I wallow in sex and booze. Dad thinks that's vile and degrading. He should talk! But man can stoop much lower than that. To harm one's fellow man is what makes man loathsome. And that's the man I am. I'm like Dad.

ALEX. No! He doesn't have a single noble thought in his head. He thinks only of money, alcohol, and women.

DOUG. A couple of months ago, he sent me twenty-five thousand in return for signing a release giving up all further claims on him.   Coincidentally, Kathryn told me that her father needed twenty-five thousand to pay off a debt right away to some shady characters. Naturally, I turned my money right over to her. One week later her father died of a heart attack. I went to the funeral, and from that moment on, I knew Kathryn loved me. We became engaged shortly thereafter.

ALEX. What happened to the twenty-five thousand?

DOUG. She returned it, and I promptly squandered it. She gave me an additional five thousand, which, she said, was a gift from her father in appreciation for my loan. Unfortunately, even as I was accepting the gift, I'd already fallen in love with Theresa.

ALEX. But you're still engaged to Kathryn, aren't you?

DOUG. Yes, but I'm breaking it off. I've already asked Theresa to marry me.

ALEX. And what did she say?

DOUG. She hasn't decided. But even so, now that I'm breaking my engagement to Kathryn, I must pay back the five thousand.

ALEX. It was a gift!

DOUG. How can I accept such a gift under the circumstances?

ALEX. Then why don't you just give it back to her? Or have you already spent it?

DOUG. No, I haven't spent it! The truth of the matter is, I've lost or misplaced it.

ALEX. (*Stands.*) What?

DOUG. Maybe in a drunken stupor. I can't remember.

ALEX. I don't believe this!

DOUG. But it's true nonetheless! So I'm going to ask Dad for the money.

ALEX. He won't give it to you.

DOUG. Legally he owes me nothing, but morally he

owes me everything.

ALEX. That's the way you see it but not the way he sees it. He won't give you anything.

DOUG. But I'm going to ask anyway. He's got five thousand on hand. I know. Melvin told me. He said that was money Dad had put aside for Theresa if she ever decided to sleep with him.

ALEX. Does Theresa know that?

DOUG. She treats it as a joke. She wouldn't sleep with him for any amount. If she went to him, there would be murder.

ALEX. Whose murder?

DOUG. His! Whose do you think? I don't intend to kill *her*.

ALEX. You wouldn't kill anyone! Surely there's some other way to get five thousand.

DOUG. Ian doesn't have that kind of money. Alex, do you?

ALEX. I don't know anyone who has that much except Dad.

DOUG. Exactly!

(*They stare at each other.*)

(*Fade-out.*)

SCENE 4

Karleton's dining room, a little later. IAN and KARLE-TON are sitting at the table. Dinner is over. GREGORY is holding a decanter of brandy, and MELVIN is pouring coffee. ALEX enters.

KARLETON. (*Happy to see* ALEX.) Here he is! My little angel! Join us! Sit down! Have you had dinner?

ALEX. (*Sitting.*) All I want is a cup of coffee.

(MELVIN *pours* ALEX *a cup of coffee.*)

KARLETON. The coffee's very good, just like the rest of the dinner. Melvin made it. He's an artist at cooking. He's also a philosopher. And when he was a boy, he liked to hang cats and then bury them with great ceremony. He also liked to examine his food for flies and cockroaches. I knew that one day he'd make a good cook. (*Pause.*) Notice he never responds to me. (*Pause.*) I think he despises and has contempt for everyone but me. Hey there, Melvin, are you human? No, not human! You grew from mildew! And that's what you are!

ALEX. Dad, stop calling him names!

KARLETON. I'm not calling him names! Melvin, do you remember when I used to call you Stinky, you little stinker?

ALEX. Dad!

KARLETON. You know, Melvin, I think you're one of those people who suddenly takes out a gun in a town square and mows down crowds of innocent people— or else blows up a building. But you'd never steal, and that's something.

MELVIN. Well, "Without God, all things are lawful." Ian taught me that. (*Pause.*) In today's newspaper, I read about a soldier who had been taken prisoner by Muslims and was threatened with agonizing death if he didn't renounce Christianity and convert to Islam. He refused. You see, the Muslims think they have the True Religion and all others are infidels. And we think we have the True Religion and all others are nonbelievers. It's for the sake of the True Religion that men torture and slay one another. And so the soldier was tortured and killed.

KARLETON. I notice, Melvin, that you always get talkative when Ian is around. What is it about him that you find so fascinating? Well, tell us, Melvin, what you think of the soldier's martyrdom.

MELVIN. I don't think it would have been a sin if the soldier had renounced his faith to save his life. What does it matter what you say publicly when no one knows what you're really thinking?

KARLETON. Ian, I do believe Melvin's trying to impress you. Give him a little praise! He even quoted you! Say something!

GREGORY. Forgive me for interrupting, but it's not so easy to renounce faith. I don't think I could.

MELVIN. (*Pointing out the window.*) Look at that mountain! The Gospels say if you have faith, you can move mountains. Well, Gregory, if you have as much faith as you say, why don't you tell that distant mountain to move to the river that runs through the town? That experiment will demonstrate that you have no more faith than I do.

　　The truth of the matter is, not one single person, from the moment Christ uttered those famous words, can move mountains. So why should God punish a poor soldier for temporarily renouncing his faith to save his life? God's mercy is famous. Surely he will forgive one soldier. (*Exits.*)

KARLETON. See! A real philosopher!

IAN. Damn it! Is this worth talking about so much?

KARLETON. Ian, I do believe you're jealous! Here, let me give you a kiss. (*He kisses* IAN *on top of his head.*) Would you like some brandy?

IAN. Yes, some brandy.

(KARLETON *takes the decanter and pours as* MARTHA *enters with a plate of cookies.*)

MARTHA. I baked a cake for Father Jeremiah and some cookies for you. Even philosophers need refreshment. (*Setting down the cookies on the table and then leaving.*)

ALEX and IAN. Thanks, Martha.

KARLETON. (*Taking a cookie and munching on it.*) Mmm, not bad. (*Pause.*) Alex, tell me, is there a God?

ALEX. (*Munching.*) Mmm, good! Yes, there's a God.

KARLETON. And a hereafter?

ALEX. Yes, and a hereafter, too. But even if there's no God and no hereafter, not all things are lawful. Father Jeremiah says that morality is independent of faith. He says there are at least as many atheists as believers who do good, and at least as many believers as athiests who do evil.

KARLETON. So there's hope for me yet! But, Ian, tell me, is there a God?

IAN. (*Munching.*) Mmm, delicious! No. There's no God.

KARLETON. And immortality?

IAN. No immortality either.

KARLETON. Not even a tiny bit? A teeny-weeny bit?

(IAN *shakes his head.*)

To think humanity has spent so much energy, caused so much misery to others, all for nothing! And yet, there must be an immortal spirit laughing at mankind, isn't there, Ian?

IAN. (*Annoyed.*) The Devil!

KARLETON. So the Devil exists!

IAN. No, the Devil doesn't exist either. We must quit the brandy! (*Stands.*)

KARLETON. Oh, just one more! A little one! (*Pours and drinks.*) Listen to me, Alex. I was rude to your Father Jeremiah today. I think he's an honorable man, I really do. But I sense he only pretends to be holy.

ALEX. Well, he does believe in God.

KARLETON. Oh no, he doesn't! Didn't you know? (*Standing.*) Everyone else seems to know—anyone with any intelligence! Why, not long ago, he told a local politician straight out, "*Credo—I believe—*but I don't know in what!"

ALEX. *Really*?

KARLETON. He really did! And furthermore, he's sensual, a regular man of the flesh. He's so sensual that I'd be afraid for my daughter—if I had a daughter. Oh, no, no! I'm confused. That isn't Father Jeremiah at all! It's another priest, one who likes altar boys. Ian, why didn't you stop me, tell me I was confused?

IAN. (*Coming back toward the table.*) I knew you'd eventually stop by yourself.

KARLETON. That's a lie! You did it on purpose! You came home to live with me, to accept my hospitality, and to spite me in my own home!

IAN. You've had too much brandy! And I think I should go!

KARLETON. I wish you would! (*Pause.*) Go! And sell the woodlands and the farm! How many times have I asked you to do that? You don't go because you want to keep an eye on me! You're afraid of Doug, afraid he might kill me! You needn't be. In spite of himself, he loves me too much to kill me.

IAN. Well, then, I'll go tomorrow, since you're so insistent on it!

KARLETON. You won't go! You're spiteful!

ALEX. Dad, stop attacking him!

KARLETON. (*Walks toward* IAN.) Ian, don't be angry.
You can sell the farm whenever you like. There's a
girl there I've had my eye on for years—the caretaker's
daughter. She's a beauty! But then, come to think of
it, I've never seen an ugly woman. You can always
find something beautiful in every woman—you just
have to know how to find it! Now that takes talent!
If God made a creature more beautiful than Woman,
he's keeping it to himself! (*Looking heavenward,
winking.*)

   Alex, what I found so attractive about your
mother besides being so beautiful was that she was so
religious. She was fond of praying to the Virgin, and
whenever she prayed, she always asked me to leave the
room. There was something between those two that
didn't include me. One night—I don't know what got
into me—(*Pantomiming.*) I took down the picture of
the Virgin and said to your mother, "You believe that
this woman—why, you believe that the picture
itself—has miraculous power. But look! I kiss her
with my tongue and nothing happens to me!" When I
did that—Good Lord!—I thought she was going to
kill me.

   (ALEX *jumps up, turns his back on*
   KARLETON, *wrings his hands, and
   visibly trembles.*)

But no! She only jumped up, wrung her hands, and
suddenly began to tremble.

   (KARLETON *walks to* ALEX, *gently turns him and
   studies him.*)

   (*In amazement.*) Alex, why, you're just like your
mother! Ian! Alex is just like his mother!

(IAN *walks to* KARLETON *so that* IAN
is on one side of KARLETON, ALEX
on the other.)

IAN. (*In anguish.*) *His* mother? *His* mother? She was
    my mother, too!
KARLETON. (*Astonished.*) *Your* mother? (*Dawn of
    recognition.*) Why, of course! (*Placing one arm
    around* ALEX, the other around IAN.) How could a
    religious fanatic have two sons so unalike, one
    religious, the other a nonbeliever?

(*Suddenly* DOUG *bursts into the room.*)

DOUG. (*Markedly agitated.*) She's here, isn't she?
    Where is she? In the bedroom? (*Running through the
    house, slamming doors, shouting.*) Melvin! Melvin?

(*Offstage, the sound of crashing dishes.*)

KARLETON. What's he doing here? Who let him in?
He intends to kill me, doesn't he? He's going to kill me!
(*To* IAN.) Don't let him kill me!

(DOUG *returns to the dining room,
followed by* MELVIN, *who stands
apart, frightened.*)

(*To* IAN.) Get him out of here!

DOUG. She's here! Where is she?

(DOUG *looks at* MELVIN *for the
answer.* DOUG *suddenly grabs* KARLE-
TON *by the shoulders and flings him to*

the floor. Then ALEX *and* GREGORY *restrain* DOUG.)

IAN. (*To* DOUG.) What are you trying to do? Kill him?
DOUG. It would serve him right! Is he any good alive?
IAN. Doug, get the hell out of here! You're drunk!

> (DOUG *turns to plead to* ALEX, *while the others attend* KARLETON *on the floor.*)

DOUG. Alex! Tell me! You're the only one I trust. Was she here just now or not?
ALEX. Doug, I swear she's not here, hasn't been here, and no one's expecting her.
IAN. She's not here, you damn fool! Go!
DOUG. (*To* KARLETON.) Well, don't expect any apologies from me, you son of a bitch! (*Runs out, slamming the door.*)

> (ALEX *and* GREGORY *help* KARLETON *into a chair.*)

KARLETON. What made him come in like that? Did he really expect to find her here? Does he really think she cares for me? Does he care for her that much? What about Kathryn? He's engaged to her. Doesn't he care about her?
ALEX. Dad, it's Theresa he loves.
KARLETON. Alex, do me a favor. Go to Theresa and tell her the money is hers if only she goes away and leaves Doug alone. I don't want her to marry him.
ALEX. Dad, there's no point! She won't take the money, and she won't give Doug up.

(Fade-out.)

SCENE 5

Church garden.   FR. IGNATIUS *and the* VISITING
PRIEST *are sitting on a bench, engaged in silent prayer.
Suddenly the* VISITING PRIEST *drops to his knees before*
FR. IGNATIUS.

FR. IGNATIUS. (*Agitated, looking about to reassure
    himself that no one is observing.*) What are you
    doing, Father?
VISITING PRIEST. I only want to bow down before you.
    I only want your blessing.
FR. IGNATIUS. (*Standing.*) Get up! Stand up at once!

> (*The* VISITING PRIEST *stands.* FR.
> IGNATIUS *rapidly makes the sign of the
> cross over him twice.*)

Be blest! Be blest! Now then, sit!

> (*They sit.*)

(*Calmly.*)   Tell me, Father, where did you say you
    were from?
VISITING PRIEST. From St. Sylvester's Church.
FR. IGNATIUS. You've come all that way just to bow
    down before me?
VISITING PRIEST. Yes! You're famous!
FR. IGNATIUS. Famous? For what?
VISITING PRIEST.   Everyone says you enjoy the
    company of angels and spirits—and that's why you
    dislike the company of people.
FR. IGNATIUS. So you're from St. Sylvester's! That
    church was built in the Middle Ages. Well, tell me,
    Father, is Sylvester well?

(*The* VISITING PRIEST *'s jaw drops.*)

Never mind! Tell me about the diet at St. Sylvester's, tell me about fasting there.

VISITING PRIEST. During Lent we don't have anything on Mondays, Wednesdays, and Fridays except water. On Tuesdays and Thursdays we eat cabbage and noodles. Saturdays we eat potatoes and peas. During Holy Week we have bread and water, and that sparingly. On Good Friday we have nothing, not even water.

FR. IGNATIUS. And what about mushrooms?

VISITING PRIEST. (*Puzzled.*) Mushrooms?

FR. IGNATIUS. Yes, sometimes that's all I eat. I go into the forest and live on mushrooms. But no one else here does that. They can't give up their earthly bread! Besides, they're in league with the Devil. Father, tell me, since you've been here, have you seen any devils?

VISITING PRIEST. (*Frightened.*) Devils? Where?

FR. IGNATIUS. I went to visit the bishop last Easter. I saw a devil sitting on a young priest's chest, hiding under his shirt with only his horns poking out. Another devil was peeking out of his pocket with sharp eyes. He was afraid of me. And there was a devil sitting on his lap, who began to play with him right there before my eyes. That priest had all those devils on him doing all those things, and he didn't even know it. I alone knew it.

VISITING PRIEST. (*Astonished.*) You can see devils?

FR. IGNATIUS. (*Angrily.*) Didn't I just tell you I could? (*Calmly.*) And when I started to leave, I saw a devil hiding behind the door. He was a big fellow with a long tail, the tip of which was in the crack of the door. So I quickly ran to the door and slammed it. He squealed and began to struggle. I made the sign of the cross, and he died on the spot. He must be rotting there and stinking. But they can't see him and they can't smell him.

VISITING PRIEST. Your words are amazing! How glad I am to have come to see you! But tell me, Father, is it true what people say, that you're in personal communication with the Holy Spirit?

FR. IGNATIUS. He does fly down to me at times.

VISITING PRIEST. In the form of a dove?

FR. IGNATIUS. Sometimes as a dove, sometimes as a sparrow or a goldfinch. And sometimes as a blue jay.

VISITING PRIEST. How do you recognize him from an ordinary blue jay?

FR. IGNATIUS. He speaks to me.

VISITING PRIEST. He speaks? In what language?

FR. IGNATIUS. Any language.

VISITING PRIEST. What does he say?

FR. IGNATIUS. Why, today, just before you came, he said a fool was about to visit me and ask silly questions.

VISITING PRIEST. Father, your words are awesome!

FR. IGNATIUS. (*Pointing.*) Look at that tree! I bet you think it's an ordinary tree, but to me it's something else.

VISITING PRIEST. What is it to you?

FR. IGNATIUS. You see those two branches? Well, they're not really branches at all. That's really Jesus Christ standing there, holding out his arms to me. He means to steal me away.

VISITING PRIEST. While you're still alive?

FR. IGNATIUS. Now you've come to my most important teaching, one I don't share with everyone. Father, you do know that you have to give up your mind for the glory of God, don't you?

(*Fade-out.*)

SCENE 6

Café, the next day. IAN *is dining alone.* THERESA *has just cleared the table and poured him some more coffee.*

IAN. Theresa, tell the truth. Are you in love with my brother Douglas, or are you just playing with him?

THERESA. (*Smiling, flirting.*) Ian, I'm in love with you. (*She kisses him on the cheek, but he withdraws.*)

(*Thoughtful.*) You take life too seriously. But if you must have an answer, I like Doug, but I haven't yet decided whether I love him.

(ALEX *enters and joins them. She lightly kisses the top of his head.*)

But *this* is the one I love above all others! It's too bad he wants to be a priest! (*Smiling, she leaves.*)

IAN. I wish I could tell whether she was serious.

ALEX. Serious? She was flirting. That's part of her charm, and one of the reasons Doug has fallen for her.

IAN. I guess so. (*Pause.*) I've finished my dinner, but go ahead and order and I'll keep you company.

ALEX. I just want dessert and coffee.

IAN. I suggest the apple pie. It's very good here. You remember how you used to love apple pie when you were little?

ALEX. You remember that? Yes, I like it still.

(THERESA *returns.*)

THERESA. Alex, love of my life, do you want to see the menu?

ALEX. No, thanks, I know what I want—apple pie and
coffee.

THERESA. (*Dramatic.*) I love a man who knows what
he wants! Oh, how I wish you wanted me! (*Still
flirting, she exits.*)

IAN. (*Shaking his head.*) You're surprised at my
remembering the apple pie. I remember everything
—except I don't remember whether I liked you.
I went off to one boarding school, and you to another.
In all those years, I confess, I never thought about you
once. And now I've been back home for more than
three months, and we've hardly said one word to each
other. But I've noticed that you look at me with
admiration.

(THERESA *brings the pie and coffee.*)

ALEX. Admiration? I love you, Ian—and Doug, too.
You were my two older brothers, whom I looked up
to and adored.

THERESA. So, Ian, I see that Alex loves you . . . and
Douglas . . . and I love Alex . . . but Alex loves apple
pie! What a predicament!

(*She strokes the back of* ALEX*'s neck
and departs.* ALEX *and* IAN *roll their
eyes as* ALEX *takes a bite of pie.*)

IAN. Well, how is it?

ALEX. Mmm. Delicious, just as you said.

IAN. You certainly appreciate the good things in life!

ALEX. It runs in the family!

(*They laugh.*)

IAN. If I were overwhelmed with disillusionment, I'd still

want to live. There's no greater gift than life. To life!

(*They joyously clink coffee cups.*)

I've often asked myself whether there's any despair
that could overcome this insatiable thirst for life, and
I've always come to the conclusion that there isn't.

ALEX. Well, I'm certainly learning a lot about you!

IAN. Is is true that you're planning to leave the seminary?

ALEX. Yes, I've decided to become part of the real world.

IAN. Which part?

ALEX. I'm thinking of becoming a high school teacher.

IAN. You'll make a good teacher! And we'll see each
other often in the real world.

ALEX. I've heard you're going out of town this weekend.

IAN. Yes, it's so. I'm going with Kathryn.

ALEX. Really?

IAN.   Doug doesn't love her. He's broken their
engagement. He loves Theresa. (*Joyously.*) If you
only knew how light my heart is now, how free! How
happy I am! I can't get Kathryn out of my mind!

ALEX. Ian, you're in love!

IAN. Yes! (*Pause.*) I've been attracted to her for a long
time. We were planning to dine here tonight, but
some matter concerning her father's estate had to be
resolved immediately. So she's with her lawyer, and
I'm here with you. I couldn't bear another evening
with Dad. In fact, I've just moved out of the house
and taken a room in town.

ALEX. And Dad?

IAN. He's glad to be rid of me. But let's not talk about
him anymore. Let's talk about the eternities.

ALEX. The "eternities"?

IAN. Yes, the eternal questions—is there a God? Is there
a hereafter? This may come as a surprise to you, but
there are times when I actually believe in God. As I

see it, if God exists, then he's completely beyond our
comprehension. But it's not so much that I don't
believe in God as that I don't like the world he has
created.

ALEX. But you just said how much you love life! So
what's wrong with the world?

IAN. I don't understand why children have to suffer. For
the sins of their fathers? That's unjust, cruel even,
and God can't be unjust and cruel. All I know is that
children suffer without reason. They're innocent!
Where's the justice in that? I demand justice now!
The suffering of children must end now! I want to see
the lamb lie down with the lion now! I want to see it
with my own eyes, to be there when everyone
understands what it's all about! I don't want to
become just another layer of topsoil for the benefit of
future generations! (*Pause.*)

If heaven is a reward for suffering, the price to get
there is too great! I want a refund! God should be
ashamed to have created such a place after what he's
put children through!

ALEX. Haven't you forgotten someone?

IAN. No, I haven't forgotten Jesus. I merely say that his
coming hasn't changed a thing where children are
concerned. Every day everywhere in the world,
innocent children still die of starvation, disease, or
accident. They're still being abused, tortured,
murdered—without committing sins. Jesus' death
solved nothing for them. (*Pause.*)

Do you know, Alex, I've written a short play about
him.

ALEX. Really?

IAN. Don't laugh! It's called (*Dramatic.*) *The Grand
Inquisitor*. It's a ridiculous thing. Do you want to
hear it?

ALEX. Yes!

SCENE 7

Café. The scene, without a break from Scene 6, contains
The Grand Inquisitor, *a play within the play.*

IAN.   (*Standing, narrating with animation.*)   My story
takes place in Seville, Spain, in the fifteenth century,
during the most terrible time of the Spanish
Inquisition, when fires were lighted daily in a
magnificent act of faith, and heretics were burned to
the glory of God, in the presence of the king and
queen, the court, the clergy, brave knights and lovely
ladies, and many of the citizens of Seville. (*Pause.*)

We are standing before the great cathedral. A
stranger appears, a young man in dusty robes, a
Christlike figure.

> (*The* STRANGER *appears upstage,
> wearing a simple hooded robe, a rope
> for a belt. His face, always turned
> upstage, is never seen by the audience.*)

The people immediately believe he is the Christ and
flock to him, some kissing his feet, others strewing
flowers before him and shouting "Hosanna!" The
Cardinal—the Grand Inquisitor—has his guard arrest
the man and immediately throw him into a dungeon
in pitch darkness.

> (*The* STRANGER *falls on his knees and
> elbows as if he has been thrown down.*)

The people bow down before the Cardinal, who
blesses them by making the sign of the cross.

(IAN *makes the sign of the cross over the audience as the* STRANGER *stands up*.)

That night the Cardinal, carrying a candle, the only light, visits the Stranger.

(*The* CARDINAL *appears upstage, carrying a burning candle*.)

The great key is placed in the lock of the iron-barred door, which is then thrown open. The Cardinal enters the cell and sets the candle down on a small table. The jail door is closed.

CARDINAL. (*Scrutinizing the* STRANGER*'s face*.) Is it *you*? Is it *really* you? Don't answer! Remain silent! I suspect it is you. (*Walking around the* STRANGER, *scrutinizing his robes and again his face*.) But what can you say? You have no right to say anything beyond that which you said of old. (*Pause*.)

Why have you come? (*Pause*.) To interfere with our work? (*Pause*.)

Tomorrow I shall condemn you and burn you at the stake as the worst of the heretics. And the very same people who today kissed your feet, threw flowers in your path, and shouted "Hosanna," tomorrow, at a sign from me (*Making the sign of the cross*.) will rush to ignite the wood.

ALEX. I don't get it. Is this a fantasy or a case of mistaken identity?

IAN. Just listen and watch! If you can't bear fantasy, then consider it a case of mistaken identity. Let me continue.

CARDINAL. (*Face-to-face with the* STRANGER.)   We
don't need you anymore! You completed your service
long ago! The church has taken over with its absolute
authority, which you gave it. You taught that
whatever we bind on earth is bound in heaven, and
that whatever we unbind is unbound. In saying that,
you gave us greater power than even you possess—or
the Father. (*Pause.*)

Do you remember when the Devil took you into the
wilderness and tempted you three times? Of course,
you do. By your responses to those three temptations,
you placed an impossible burden on man. You
expected him to make the same choices as you. You
gave man a freedom that is impossible. Let me
remind you. It's been a long time. (*Pause.*)

First the Devil took you into the desert for forty
days. You had no food. At last he took you out of
the desert. You were hungry. He said quite
reasonably, "Eat some bread. Refresh yourself. Here
are stones. Turn them into bread and eat." "No!" you
said, quoting Scripture, "Man does not live by bread
alone but by every word that comes from the mouth of
God." (*Pause.*)

You were starving, and all you could do at a time
like that was to quote Scripture! In doing that, you
set a very bad example. Well, it doesn't matter. We
know that starving people cannot turn to God before
their stomachs are full. So we feed them, and they lay
their freedom at our feet. We have corrected your
mistake. And we declare that we are doing this *in
your name.* (*Pause.*)

By your example, you taught man that he had the
freedom to do what is right under the harshest
circumstances. But how many can behave righteously
under *ordinary* circumstances? The truth is, man does

not want freedom under *any* circumstances. Man wants to be told what to believe and what not to believe, what to do and what not to do. (*Smiles.*) So we tell him, and he is happy. (*Pause.*)

The church in her wisdom has taken away your impossible freedom. And she has done so for mankind's own good. But don't worry! The people don't even realize they prefer slavery to freedom! (*Pause.*)

Why, then, have you come to interfere with all the good we are doing? (*Pause.*)

Then the Devil tempted you a second time. He took you to Jerusalem and set you on the highest pinnacle of the Temple and said, "Jump! Ordinary men would perish on hitting the ground from such a great height, but you will not die. You will stand up without so much as a scratch or bruise and brush yourself off. You will have performed a great miracle before all the people, and they will be amazed and instantly believe in you." But again you refused! You despised miracles! You insisted that only sinful and evil people wanted miracles! You wanted people to have faith in God without miracles. And you quoted Scripture again: "You shall not tempt the Lord your God." (*Pondering.*)

Why do you have such a limited understanding of people? They love miracles! You cannot have religion without miracles! Well, we have rectified your mistake. We have given the faithful more miracles than they can possibly imagine. And they love us for them. And do you know what? They would never believe in you without miracles! (*Pause.*)

Why have you come to disturb our work? (*Pause.*)

Then the Devil tempted you a third time. He set you on top of the tallest mountain and showed you all the kingdoms of the world. And he said, "All these I will give to you. All I ask is that you worship me." And you said indignantly, "You shall worship the Lord your God, and him only shall you serve." And then you said angrily, "Be gone, Satan!" And the Devil, having had quite enough of you, departed, not because he thought he had failed, but because he knew the church would listen. (*Pause.*)

You made Peter leader. And shortly after he became leader, you became angry at him and said, "Get behind me, Satan!" Only much later did some people begin to realize what name you had called him! But by then it was too late! Yes! The church joined forces with the Devil! And as our first reward, he gave us the city of Rome! (*Crescendo.*) And then he gave us the Roman Empire! And then we took up the sword of Caesar and went on to conquer the world! (*Pause.*) You were wrong to reject the world. (*Pause.*) The church has rectified your mistake. (*Pause.*)

Finally, what did you do when the going got rough? (*Sighing.*) You died! But we shall not die. You said, "The gates of hell shall not prevail against us." True! The gates of hell have become *part* of us! We reject nothing that enhances our power. And the faithful love us for our power. We make all the rules that allow them to live without a care in the world. We have the answer to every question. What *we* say makes the people secure. What *you* said only troubled them. But don't worry. We still make you central to our worship. (*Making the sign of the cross.*) The faithful love you more now than they did when you came the first time and acted without our help. (*Pause.*)

We will not let you come between us and them. (*Turning to the audience.*)

You see, with our way, the faithful think they are
going to heaven even when they are not. (*Smiling.*)
We tell them that all they have to do is believe in you
and trust in us. What's the difference whether they go
to heaven or not, so long as they think they're going?
(*Smiling.*)

Your way was the narrow way, only for the strong
and courageous. There aren't too many of them. Our
way is for everyone. You said the meek shall inherit
the earth, but you didn't say how. How could the
meek and the weak do it without us? You see, it's
not you but we who truly love the weak. Does it
matter that they are not following the narrow path of
salvation of which you spoke? (*Pause.*)

The people love us because of the broad highways
we have paved, the colossal cathedrals we have built,
and the great spectacles we have created. Have you
ever seen the coronation or the funeral of a pope? No,
of course you haven't. You hated spectacles. You
hated funerals, even simple ones. Well, we put on the
greatest shows on earth, and you know what? The
faithful love them! Bread and circuses! The people
don't realize that those things count for nothing
according to your teachings because according to our
teachings they count for *everything*! And our
teachings is what matters! (*Pause.*)

Why have you come to interfere with our work?
(*Pause.*)

Tomorrow you will be led out and tied to the stake
and burned in the square before the great cathedral,
along with others of your people and all the other
heretics. You shall become a martyr again, just as
you were of old. But this time the faithful will learn
that your martyrdom was not for the vast majority of
poor souls who are so devoted to you, who adore you
so, who love you so. Tomorrow you shall be

punished for what you really are, a friend of the elect and an enemy of the people! (*Pause.*)

Yesterday in the public square, we burned one hundred heretics at the stake, many of them Jews, your own flesh and blood. Those people, *your people*, are troublemakers and always have been. You are a true son of a troublemaking people! No wonder you were killed! No wonder your people are always being killed! Their continued existence is an ever-present reminder that the freedom you taught actually exists. Their existence teaches others that not everyone has a need to believe the things we say and teach. That is a dangerous message, a divisive message, one that gets the faithful agitated. And so we have to burn the Jews and the heretics at the stake. What other choice do we have? You will be burned with them because you are the worst of the heretics! (*Pause.*)

I have nothing more to say. Do you have anything to say for yourself? No. How could you?

> (*For several moments, the* STRANGER *continues to stand where he's been all along, facing the* CARDINAL. *Now he walks up to the* CARDINAL *and kisses him. The* CARDINAL *is stunned.*)

What have you done? Shown love to your enemy? I can't bear that! I can bear anything but that! (*Contemptuously.*) I don't want your love, because I don't love you! (*Thinking.*) Mmm. I won't burn you tomorrow. I've changed my mind! To make a martyr of you again would be a mistake—a *perilous* mistake. So I've decided to let you live and go free. Yes! I'll set you free this very instant. (*Opening the door.*) Go! You are free!

(*The* STRANGER *departs.*)

(*The* CARDINAL *shouts after him.*) Just remember!
We no longer need you! So never come again! Never!
Never!

(*The candle is extinguished, and the*
CARDINAL *vanishes.*)

ALEX. But I don't understand! Your play is in praise of
Jesus! That's not what you intended!

IAN. Things don't always turn out as you intended.

ALEX. What happened to the prisoner?

IAN. He walked out of jail a free man. He walked
through the dark alleys of the town to the outskirts
and went away.

ALEX. And the Grand Inquisitor?

IAN. (*Lightheartedly.*) The kiss still glows in his heart.

ALEX. Why, it's all nonsense, nothing but nonsense! A
senseless play by a senseless author!

IAN. (*Concerned.*) And here I thought that after you had
heard my little play you'd love me even more! But I
see I was wrong! Are you going to denounce and
disown me?

(ALEX *walks to* IAN *and kisses him.*
IAN *grins.*)

(*Happily.*) You stole that right from my play! That's
plagiarism!

(*Fade-out.*)

SCENE 8

Karleton's garden, later that evening. KARLETON is seated on the bench in pajamas, slippers, and a white robe. He lifts a flask from the robe pocket and takes a swig. ALEX enters. KARLETON replaces the flask.

KARLETON. Why are you here?

ALEX. Well, Ian went off, leaving you alone, and I wanted to see how you were doing.

KARLETON. Yes, Ian's moved out, got his own place in town, and run off, not to sell the woodlands and the farm but to be with Kathryn! I think he's out to steal Doug's fiancée!

ALEX. That's ridiculous. She's no longer Doug's fiancée. They broke their engagement. Ian has every right to go off with her if he wants. He loves her, and I think she loves him.

KARLETON. (*Standing.*) Was that the reason Ian came home? To get Kathryn for himself?

ALEX. Why do you say that when you know he came home to help make peace between you and Doug?

KARLETON. Perhaps you're right. One thing is certain: Ian's never asked me for money. That's good, because he won't get any. I intend to live as long as possible and carry on my sins to the end. That takes money. (*Pause.*)

    Alex, don't believe what they teach at the seminary. Let me give you a real lesson in life. Sin is sweet. All men engage in it, and there isn't one who doesn't like it. That's why they repeat it over and over again. They may feel guilty about it, but you can learn to live with guilt, you really can. (*Sits.*)

    Do you know, Alex, not all priests like boys. Some prefer men. And some even like women. In the next town, there's a house shared by several

women. The townspeople call them the "priests'
wives." I know because I've been there myself,
passing myself off as a priest. Thank God there's
nothing of the sort in our town!

ALEX. Dad, stop! What I'm going to say now has
nothing to do with anything you've just said. But I
know you'll be happy to learn I'm leaving the
seminary. I've decided to become a schoolteacher.

KARLETON. Oh, thank God! I knew you'd come to
your senses! (*Embracing and kissing* ALEX.) Alex,
the only difference between me and other men is that I
sin openly, whereas most do it on the sly.

Now that brings me to Ian again. After all is said
and done, he's really just a conceited fool. He never
talks about anything important, anything real. At
least not to me. Ian's a tomb, a riddle, a sphinx. He
must be hiding some deep secret. That's why he likes
to talk only about the hereafter.

But, you know, you can talk about the hereafter
until you're blue in the face. You can go to theology
school. You can pray all day long your entire life.
But in the end, you won't know any more than you
did in the beginning. What's the purpose of it? And
while you're thinking, (*Pulling out the flask.*) would
you like some brandy?

ALEX. No, and I don't think you should have any more
either.

KARLETON. You're right—as usual. (*Taking a swig.*)

ALEX. Well, I've got to go.

(ALEX *stands and kisses him.*)

KARLETON. (*Surprised.*) What's that for? We'll see
each other again. Or do you think we won't?

ALEX. I didn't mean anything by it.

KARLETON. That's good! Good-bye, then. Come again

soon. What about tomorrow? Yes, come tomorrow!

ALEX. (*Smiling.*) Yes, tomorrow. (*He leaves.*)

KARLETON. (*Staring at the flask.*) I won't drink any
more, at least not today. Mmm. Well, let's not be
too hasty! (*Taking a swig.*)

(*Fade-out.*)

SCENE 9

*Fr. Jeremiah's bedroom.   FR. JEREMIAH is on his
deathbed, propped up by several pillows, and surrounded
by* ALEX, DR. HART, FR. IGNATIUS, and the
VISITING PRIEST.

DR. HART. (*Applying a stethoscope to* FR. JERE-
MIAH*'s chest, then removing it. Announcing softly.*)
His heart is failing rapidly.

FR. JEREMIAH. (*Short of breath.*) Paradise! Life itself
is paradise, and we're already in paradise, but few
people know it. If everyone knew it, we could have
heaven on earth today. Well, tomorrow then, because
it requires something. It requires that all people care
for one another, help one another, serve one another.

We're all responsible for everyone else, and for the
earth, too. The problem is, few people act as if they
knew that. If everyone knew it, the world would be
paradise at once. (*Pause.*)

The glory of God is everywhere—trees and fields,
mountains and lakes, sea and sky. We must love all
of God's creation, love the world. I have sinned. I
have not noticed God's glory enough. I hope God
will forgive me for my great sin. (*Pause.*)

Alex, (*Pause.*)

(ALEX *kneels, then takes* FR. JERE-
MIAH*'s hand.*)

I think you should leave the seminary. You're not
happy here. You should become a schoolteacher.
You'd be happy doing that. Men are meant to be
happy. Even a happy man has the right to say, "I,
too, am doing God's will." (*Pause.*)

Dear friends, my life is ending. Let me share with
you what I've learned. Salvation? There's only one
way to salvation. Make yourself responsible for all
men. All men are brothers, and we're all servants of
one another. To serve humanity is to know paradise.
As for hell, it doesn't exist. The only hell is the
suffering that comes from being unable to love.
(*Clutching chest and dying.*)

DR. HART. (*Applying stethoscope to* FR. JEREMIAH*'s
chest.* Announcing.) He's gone.

FR. IGNATIUS. (*Unexpectedly standing and ranting.*)
Casting out, I cast out! Casting out, I cast out!
(*Making the sign of the cross repeatedly in a direction
away from the body as he performs an exorcism on
the dead man.*)

(The VISITING PRIEST, *terrified, falls
to his knees and prays silently, crossing
himself repeatedly.* ALEX *stands beside*
DR. HART, *both looking on in
astonishment.*)

Satan, go hence! Satan, go hence! Casting out, I cast
out! (*Although the exorcism is now over, the rant
continues.*)

The dead man was no saint. He taught that life was
a joy, not a vale of tears. He didn't believe in hell.

He didn't believe in salvation through Jesus Christ. And so hosts of demons have invaded this room like spiders. They're in all the corners. (*Sniffing audibly.*) Already his body is beginning to rot and stink, and in that we have a great sign from God. (*Pause.*)

The dead man did not fast. He loved his appetites, worshipped them, and satisfied them abundantly. He had tea every afternoon with cake and cookies. And he enjoyed the company of the women who made and brought the baked goods to him.

(*Turning to* ALEX *and* DR. HART, *accusingly.*) But worst of all, he worshipped learning. Learned men! Christ hated them all! You two are so clever. You think you are so superior. I came here with little learning, and whatever I knew I've forgotten.

(*Falling to his knees, arms raised and outstretched, ecstatic and victorious.*) The evil one is dead! My God has conquered! Christ has conquered!

(*Fade-out.*)

SCENE 10

Mrs. Holiday's living room. There is a knock. MRS. HOLIDAY *goes to the door and opens it.*

MRS. HOLIDAY. Douglas Karleton! I had a feeling all morning that you were coming, and here you are! Father Jeremiah died. Did you know that?

DOUG. No, this is the first I've heard of it. But, Mrs. Holiday, I can't think of anything except myself right now. I'm desperate. And if you don't help me, I don't know what I'll do.

MRS. HOLIDAY.   Darling, I know! I knew of your
  despair before you told me.   I've been thinking about
  you a long time.   When your poor mother died—
  what a tragedy! How I adored her! How beautiful she
  was! When she entered a room, all eyes turned to her.
  I'd have done anything for her.

DOUG. If that is so, I hope you'll help me. It's a matter
  of life or death. Let me get right to the point.

MRS. HOLIDAY.   No, my dear, no explanations are
  necessary. Let's sit first.

(*They sit. She moves too close to him.*)

There, that's better. As for helping you, you're not
  the first man I've helped. You must have heard of my
  cousin's husband. He was ruined, utterly ruined. So
  I advised him to take up horse breeding.   You
  wouldn't believe how well he's doing now. Do you
  know anything about horses?

DOUG. No, nothing at all. But, Mrs. Holiday, I need
  five thousand immediately. I beg you to lend it to
  me. You're the only one I can turn to.

MRS. HOLIDAY. Oh, darling, tell me all that later! You
  ask for five thousand, but I can give you
  immeasurably more!

DOUG.   But I don't need more. I only need five
  thousand.

MRS. HOLIDAY. Enough! It's as good as done! I
  promised to help you, and help you I shall! What do
  you think of the goldfields?

DOUG. Goldfields? I've never thought about them at all.

MRS. HOLIDAY. But I have! I've been watching you
  for over a month, and you have no idea how many
  times I thought, "That's a man who ought to go to the
  goldfields."   I've studied the way you walk and
  concluded, "This is a man who would find gold."

DOUG. You drew that conclusion from the way I walk?

MRS. HOLIDAY. Of course, from your walk! Surely
you didn't think I came to that conclusion from your
character!

DOUG. But the five thousand you so generously promised to lend me a moment ago?

MRS. HOLIDAY. No, my sweet! Much more! I'm
going to make you rich! You'll make a fortune from
gold. We can't leave it all to the Jews, can we? And
as a result of your new great wealth, you will found
institutions that will be named for you. You'll help
the poor, and they will bless you. You will become
famous!

DOUG. Perhaps we can talk about that another time.

MRS. HOLIDAY. Tell me, will you go to the goldfields
or not? Answer me, yes or no!

DOUG. I'll go—afterwards. But for now—

MRS. HOLIDAY. (*Jumping up.*) Wait! (*Running to a
dresser, pulling out drawers and rifling them one
after another.*) Wait! I'm sure it's here! Wait!

DOUG. (*Standing. Aside.*) The five thousand! What a
splendid woman! If only she didn't talk so much!

MRS. HOLIDAY. Here! (*Pulling a brown envelope from
a drawer.*) Here is what I was looking for!

> (*Excitedly she gives the envelope to*
> DOUG, *who, overjoyed, rips it open. A
> puzzled look comes over his face as he
> removes a religious medal on a chain.
> He searches the envelope for something
> more but finds nothing. She takes the
> necklace from him. Baffled, he contin-
> ues to hold the envelope.*)

The medal once belonged to a saint. What was his
name? Oh, it doesn't matter! Let me put it on you

and consecrate you to a new life and a new career!

> (*She puts the chain around his neck and tucks the medal under his shirt, caressing his chest while doing so.*)

There! Now you are ready to begin!

DOUG. I am touched, deeply touched! I can't thank you enough!

MRS. HOLIDAY. Goldfields are just what you want, and there's no place for women there! Kathryn isn't the woman for you. She belongs with Ian, who is so intelligent, so charming, and so chivalrous. And Theresa's not right for you, either. She is so vulgar, while you are so dashing and unpredictable. Afterward, when you return from the goldfields rich and famous, you'll find the woman of your dreams. Your interest in women will have ripened, and wealthy women will pop up everywhere!

DOUG. But that's not the point!

MRS. HOLIDAY. Oh, my darling, yes it is! That's exactly the point, even though you don't realize it.

DOUG. You'll make me weep.

MRS. HOLIDAY. Oh, weep, my boy, weep! How I love to see a man cry! Now you must go, you really must.

> (*Taking him by the arm, escorting him to the door.*)

And do hurry back from the goldfields and share your happiness with me! And at last you shall find a woman worthy of you!

DOUG. But, Mrs. Holiday, for the last time, are you going to give me the money you promised?

MRS. HOLIDAY. Money? What money?

DOUG. The five thousand!

MRS. HOLIDAY. Five thousand? I don't have a penny. I've just had to borrow one thousand myself. And even if I did have it, I certainly wouldn't lend it to you. First of all, lending money to friends means losing friends. Second, I wouldn't give it to you because I want to save you from yourself. Trust me! I've studied you, and I know what's best for you!

DOUG. (*Shouting angrily.*) Jesus Christ! (*He throws down the envelope and storms out, slamming the door.*)

(MRS. HOLIDAY *stands frightened and trembling.*)

(*Fade-out.*)

SCENE 11

Café, later that day. THERESA *is setting a table, her back to the door.* DOUG *enters unobserved; ecstatic, he runs to her, lifts her by the waist, and spins her about. She smiles radiantly. He sets her down and kisses her passionately.*

THERESA. (*Happy.*) What are you doing here?

DOUG. I want to celebrate! Let's get a bottle of champagne!

(*He hums some bars from* "Ode to Joy." *He hugs and kisses her again.*)

THERESA. (*Laughing but puzzled.*) What are we celebrating?

DOUG. (*Beaming.*) Me! Us! (*Suddenly serious.*) Where
were you earlier today? I came by looking for you.

THERESA.   My aunt caught a cold, and I brought her
some soup. She's doing much better now.   But tell
me, please, what are we celebrating?

DOUG. My happiness! Our happiness!

> (*He takes her by the hand, as if they
> were dancing, and twirls her under his
> arm.*)

THERESA.   To what do we owe this newfound
happiness?

DOUG. (*Pulling out a wad of bills.*) To this!

THERESA. (*Astonished.*) Where did you get that? It
looks like a lot!

DOUG. Five thousand, to be exact! (*Stuffing the wad
back into his pocket.*)

THERESA. Did you find a goldfield?

DOUG. (*Laughing.*) I know a woman who is very fond
of goldfields—Mrs. Holiday!

THERESA. Did that silly woman lend you the money?

DOUG. No, it's mine, I swear it!

THERESA. (*Dubious.*) Tell me the truth! Did you steal
it from your father?

DOUG. (*Annoyed.*) No, I didn't steal it.   What do you
take me for, a thief? I'd *kill* him before I'd *steal* from
him! It's *mine*! (*Grinning.*) It really is! Now I've
got the money to give back to Kathryn!

THERESA. (*Joyfully.*) Well, what are you waiting for?
Give it to her! (*Holding him close.*) Then we'll go
away from here, start life anew. (*Dubious.*)   You
don't love her anymore, do you? (*Laughing.*) If you
do, I'll strangle her!

DOUG. (*Wrapping his arms around her.*) No, you're the
only one I love!

THERESA. (*Eyes closed, smiling, arms still wrapped around him.*) Take me to the ends of the earth, and there we can begin a new life together! I love you.

> (*The café piano player, unseen, begins to play the main melody to an early twentieth-century American standard such as "You Made Me Love You" or "It Had to Be You."* DOUG *and* THERESA *dance for several moments. The music continues to the end of the scene, softly during dialogue.*)

DOUG. (*Suddenly serious, stops dancing and steps back from* THERESA.) And my father?
THERESA. I never cared for your father. Only one man fills my heart—you! You are my joy!—my stars and moon! You are my god! You are my life! I love you madly!

> (*She kisses him. He is reassured and happy. They resume dancing.*)

DOUG. Your face has haunted me every waking minute of every day. One day she'll be mine, I thought. And now it's happening!

> (*While dancing, they kiss long and passionately. The* POLICE CAPTAIN *enters unobserved. He watches them a moment with enjoyment. Then, without sentiment, he approaches them and taps* DOUG *on the shoulder.*)

POLICE CAPTAIN. Are you Douglas Karleton?

(THERESA *and* DOUG *stop dancing, puzzled and frightened.*)

DOUG. I am.

POLICE CAPTAIN. (*Flashing a badge, then pulling out handcuffs.*) Douglas Karleton, you are under arrest. You have been charged with the robbery and murder of your father.

(THERESA *and* DOUG *are stunned. The* POLICE CAPTAIN *pulls back* DOUG*'s hands, clamps on handcuffs, and begins to lead him out.* THERESA *looks at* DOUG *puzzled.* DOUG *looks at her bewildered. The* POLICE CAPTAIN *and* DOUG *exit as the music swells.*)

(*Fade-out.*)

INTERMISSION

ACT II

SCENE 1

Doug's prison cell. DOUG *is sitting on a cot, head in hands. The* GUARD, *accompanying Doug's lawyer, the* DEFENDER, *unlocks the barred door.*

GUARD. Doug, your lawyer is here. (*The* DEFENDER *enters the cell. The* GUARD *locks the door and leaves.*)

DOUG. (*Looking up, standing.*) I often wanted to, but I didn't kill him. So who did? How did he die?

DEFENDER. He was found on his bedroom floor, lying face down in a pool of blood, his head bashed in by a poker.

DOUG. How horrible!

DEFENDER. If it's any consolation, the coroner says he probably died instantly. Why did you hate your father?

DOUG. (*Pacing.*) I couldn't bear the sight of him—irreverent, loathsome, trampling on everything sacred. I hated him.

DEFENDER. Why did you need five thousand?

DOUG. To pay back a debt.

DEFENDER. To whom?

DOUG. I'd rather not talk about it.

DEFENDER. Were you in his garden the night he died?

DOUG. Yes.

DEFENDER. When you were there—and this is important—was the bedroom door to the garden open?

DOUG. No, it was shut.

DEFENDER. Are you certain?

DOUG. As certain as I am that we're talking. Why do you ask?

DEFENDER. The police found the door wide open.

DOUG. Who opened it? My father didn't. He was too afraid to leave the door open, afraid of me. If the door was open, the killer opened it.

DEFENDER. The prosecution believes that the killer entered through that door and, after committing the crime, left by the same door.

DOUG. I only watched my father through the window. I didn't go into the bedroom. And the door *was* shut.

DEFENDER. Why were you watching? What were you looking for?

DOUG. I wanted to reassure myself that Theresa wasn't with him.

DEFENDER. Why? Was she customarily in his bedroom?

DOUG. No! But my father invited her home once. He offered her five thousand if she'd sleep with him.

DEFENDER. That's a lot of money. Did she take him up on his offer?

DOUG. (*Angrily.*) No! But I had to see that for myself. That's why I entered the garden and peered through the window. (*Controlled.*) She wasn't at work that day. She'd gone off to see a sick aunt, but I didn't know that at the time. (*Embarrassed.*) I was afraid she was taking my father up on his offer. But as soon as I saw how mistaken I was, I felt ashamed and left. I was also deliriously happy that I'd been wrong.

DEFENDER. Your father wouldn't have opened the door to anyone?

DOUG. He would have opened it to Theresa, but he never got the chance. And he would have opened it to—

DEFENDER. To—?

DOUG. Melvin, my half brother, my illegitimate half brother. *And* he would have opened it to Gregory and to my brothers—but never to me.

DEFENDER. Who do you think killed your father?

DOUG. I keep thinking it's Melvin. But that's

impossible! He's soft as a kitten. Couldn't it have been a burglar?

DEFENDER. The police inspector said there was no sign of forced entry.

DOUG. Well, I'm not going to say it was Melvin. Do you suspect him?

DEFENDER. No one is above suspicion.

DOUG. From the instant I learned of the murder, I thought of Melvin. But I keep suppressing it.

DEFENDER. Why? Why can't it be Melvin?

DOUG. Because he's a coward. Whenever he's with me, he's afraid I might strike him, even though I've never raised a hand to him. An eight-year-old could beat him up. Once, when I put my arm around him, I thought he was going to die. He became tense and terrified and began to tremble.

DEFENDER. I don't think that shows he's afraid of you.

DOUG. What motive could he have for killing my father —*his* father? He doesn't care at all about money. No, it isn't Melvin.

DEFENDER. Many people would kill their own father. Many people think you killed your own father. That's what this is all about.

DOUG. (*Angrily.*) It's pretty low of you to say that. You are, after all, my attorney, and I've already told you I didn't kill him.

DEFENDER. I believe you, but where did you get the five thousand?

DOUG. The answer to that question would expose me to greater disgrace than murdering and robbing my father —*if* I had murdered and robbed him.

DEFENDER. You have very high standards of disgrace.

DOUG. Maybe so.

DEFENDER. Gregory said in his deposition that the bedroom door was wide open as you ran from the garden.

DOUG. He is mistaken. He is an old man, and he is wrong.

DEFENDER. He refuses to budge.

DOUG. So do I!

DEFENDER. An empty envelope with the name Theresa in your father's handwriting was found on your father's bedroom floor.

DOUG. Then, Melvin *was* the killer! No one else knew where my father hid that envelope.

DEFENDER. *You* didn't know?

DOUG. No! Melvin told me about an envelope with money for Theresa. But he didn't tell me *where* the envelope was hidden. It's all clear to me now. Melvin must have killed him after I'd run away and while Gregory was lying drunk in the garden. That stinking dog! God will kill him! You'll see!

DEFENDER. I have to ask you again, and this time I must have an answer. Your life depends on it. Where did you get the five thousand?

DOUG. Since you must know, the money was my own.

DEFENDER. Your *own*?

DOUG. I know it sounds preposterous. I stuffed it under my underwear in my dresser several weeks ago. I forgot where I'd hidden it. I thought I'd lost or squandered it, but I found it yesterday when I was searching for a pair of shorts. I was startled to find the money, but then I remembered I'd hidden it there.

DEFENDER. You forgot where you'd hidden five thousand?

DOUG. I was drunk when I hid it.

DEFENDER. Not a bad hiding place for a drunk.

DOUG. I'm more clever drunk than sober.

DEFENDER. Where did you get that money in the first place?

DOUG. From her.

DEFENDER. From whom?

DOUG. Kathryn, my former fiancée. I'm ashamed to drag her into this. She gave me five thousand as a token of her father's esteem for me and in preparation for our forthcoming marriage. Oh, this is so hard, and now comes the hardest part. She gave it to me on the very day I discovered I was in love with Theresa, and still I didn't refuse the gift. And that is why I'm a good-for-nothing. That night I got drunk and hid the money on the chance that Theresa would tell me she loved me as much as I loved her, in which case I intended to give the five thousand back to Kathryn. And that's what I plan to do.

DEFENDER. Well, I'm glad you told me. (*Standing.*) Now I must go. (*Shouting.*) Guard!

DOUG. (*Standing.*) I didn't kill him!

DEFENDER. Douglas, I'll fight for you and do everything I can to defend you.

(*Fade-out.*)

SCENE 2

Melvin's room. The bed is more or less parallel to the footlights. MELVIN is in bed, coughing occasionally. There is a night table at the side and a stool at the foot of the bed. He is deeply engrossed in reading. IAN enters. MELVIN continues to read.

IAN. (*Softly.*) Melvin.

> (MELVIN *looks up and puts the book on the night table.*)

Hello. I came by to see how you're doing.

MELVIN. (*Coolly.*) Oh. hello. I'm fine. I had pneumonia, but I'm getting over it.

IAN. That's good.

MELVIN. So you come to see me at last!

IAN. I heard you were ill.

MELVIN. So you come to see me because I was ill. (*Pause.*) Well, I never thought it would end like this. I mean, I never thought it would end with Karleton's murder. Who would have thought Doug would actually do it?

IAN. (*Annoyed.*) You are a clever one!

MELVIN. You've always known that. We're really very much alike. We're practically twins! We were born the same year, the same day.

IAN. Doug accuses you of the murder and the theft.

MELVIN. He's only trying to save himself.

IAN. Well, I don't suspect you at all. And I'm glad you're feeling better. Now I've got to go. I'll come again. Is there anything you want, anything I can get you?

MELVIN. Martha brings me everything I need. And people who care about me visit every day.

> (IAN *turns to go, walking toward the door.*)

Before you go, I want to say something about the murder.

> (*He sits up in bed.* IAN *sharply turns to face him.*)

As for murdering him, you couldn't have done it. But as for wanting someone to do it, that was just what you wanted.

IAN. Why should I have wanted it?

MELVIN. The inheritance. After Karleton's death, you stood to inherit a fortune, each of you. Of course the will isn't going to be read until after the trial. And when Doug is found guilty, you and Alex will split his share.

IAN. (*Walking to the foot of the bed, angrily.*) So, according to you, I wanted Doug to do it! I was counting on him to do it! If I had counted on anyone to do it, I would have counted on you!

MELVIN. (*Gleefully.*) I always thought you were counting on me.

IAN. I feel like punching you in the mouth!

MELVIN. (*Shrinking.*) Under ordinary circumstances, people don't do that nowadays. But under extraordinary circumstances, they still resort to it.

IAN. Look, I'm not afraid of you or your insinuations! You can say whatever you like about me. But tomorrow in court, I'll unmask you for what you are!

MELVIN. You'd better keep your mouth shut, because I could do the same to you!

IAN. You're threatening me?

MELVIN. Even if the court doesn't believe everything I'll say, the public will. And you'll be humiliated. I'm talking about the murder, of course.

IAN. I knew you were talking about the murder. What else would you be talking about? And yes, you're right! I hoped for the murder. I wanted the murder. But the murder I wanted was yours!

MELVIN. You seem ill. You don't look yourself. Your eyeballs are yellow.

IAN. It's not *my* health I've come to talk about.

MELVIN. Why do you torment me? You've always tormented me, even when we were the best of friends.

IAN. We were never the best of friends! I've had nothing to do with you! (*Trembling.*)

MELVIN. Why are you so upset? Because of the trial?

Don't worry. Nothing will happen to you. Go home.
Go to bed. Get some sleep. And don't be afraid of
anything.

IAN. (*Trembling more visibly.*) What have I to be afraid
of?

MELVIN. (*Sitting straight up in bed.*) It's strange that
such an intelligent man should play such a farce! But
I repeat, you've nothing to be afraid of. I won't say a
word. No one has any proof. But look how your
hands are trembling! Go home! You didn't murder
him.

IAN. I know that.

MELVIN. Really? Well, then, I have to tell you that it
was actually you who did murder him!   You
understood that before, and you understand it now.

IAN. The only thing I understand is that you are out of
your mind!

MELVIN. Aren't you growing tired of this game? Here
we are alone. What's the point of keeping up this
pretense? Are you still trying to blame *me*? *You*
murdered him! I was only your instrument, your
faithful servant. And it was out of love for you that I
did it.

IAN. (*Astonished, sitting down on the stool.*) *You* did it?
You *really* did?

MELVIN. You really didn't know?

IAN. (*Standing, angry.*) You're a raving lunatic, and
you're lying when you say you killed him! You are
trying to torment me.

MELVIN. Wait! (*Opening the drawer of the night table
and removing folded bills of money held by a paper
clip.*) What have we here? The money—all five
thousand! You don't need to count it. Take it!

> (*He places the money in* IAN*'s hand.*
> IAN *looks at it incredulously, slips it*

into his pocket, and almost collapses onto the stool. MELVIN continues gleefully.)

Now you know for sure! Didn't you really know until now?

IAN. No. All along I thought it was Doug. Did you kill him all by yourself or with Doug's help?

MELVIN. Not with Doug's help. Doug is completely innocent. (*Joyously.*) I did it all alone. Well, not entirely alone. It was also with you.

IAN. Why am I trembling so?

MELVIN. You used to be so bold! But now how frightened you are!

IAN. Because I finally realize you really did kill him.

MELVIN. (*Sitting back in bed.*) I killed him, but you are the murderer!

IAN. Tell me how you did it! Tell me everything!

MELVIN. (*Sitting up.*) It was late at night. Something awakened me, shouting noises in the garden, Martha's snoring. I went out the back door by my room into the garden. Gregory was lying there on the ground, drunk and singing. I looked in through the bedroom window. I could see Karleton drinking. (*Pause.*)

I returned by the back door and walked through the house to his bedroom. By then I'd decided to kill him, but I didn't know how. (*Pause.*)

I entered his room. I was surprised he wasn't happy to see me. "You're going to leave me, aren't you?" he said. "Running off to another city and opening a restaurant? You ungrateful bastard! You shitty dog of a shitty mother!" By now I was shaking more with rage than with fear. He stood up, turning his back to me, and I knew the moment had come. (*Pause.*)

I picked up the poker by the fireplace and swung it with all my might down on his head. (*Smiling.*) I

could hear the skull cracking. He didn't cry out, just
fell to the floor, blood pouring from his head, but not
one drop on me. I took the handkerchief from my
pocket and wiped any fingerprints from the handle,
then dropped the poker on the floor next to the body.
Next I took down the painting over the fireplace,
found the envelope on the back tucked in the frame,
removed it, put the painting back, ripped open the
envelope, and took the money. (*Pause.*) What to do
with the envelope? Take it? No. Drop it on the floor.
Then it would look like a case of murder done for
robbery by a careless thief. No one has ever called me
careless. (*Gleefully.*) People would think of Doug.
(*Pause.*)

I then opened the door from the bedroom to the
garden so that people would think the killer ran off
that way. Gregory was still lying out there singing. I
walked through the house back to my bed. Fate was
kind: Martha was still snoring. Once in bed, I
coughed loudly, quite unintentionally. I was coming
down with pneumonia.   My coughing must have
awakened her.   Not seeing Gregory in bed, she ran
into the garden. You know the rest.

IAN. I'm dumbfounded.

MELVIN.   You ran off with Kathryn the day of the
    murder, but didn't I tell you not to go?   You
    suspected that with you gone, Karleton would be
    murdered, so you ran off, permitting the murder to
    happen. You wanted it to happen and set things up,
    so what's the difference whether you actually murdered
    him or not? I know that, but you refuse to know it.

IAN. (*Standing.*) Why can't you speak plainly?

MELVIN (*Getting out of bed and standing facing* IAN.)
    I am speaking plainly! You simply refuse to listen!
    Let me repeat. You murdered him. I was merely your
    instrument. I only did what you wanted me to do. I

would have done anything for you, and you knew
that. And now you're going to be very rich!

IAN. I didn't put you up to it. It was your own idea.
You did it without any input from me. Tomorrow in
court I'll tell everything. Everything!

> (*He takes* MELVIN *firmly by the arm.*)

And you must confess. You must!

> (MELVIN *places his hand on* IAN's
> *brow.* IAN *pushes him away.*)

MELVIN. Ian, you're ill. You've got a fever. (*Pause.*)
If you tell the things I told you, I'll deny ever having
said them. I'll say you're only saying those things
because you're trying to save your brother's life. And
what proof will you have?

IAN. (*Holding up the money.*) This!

MELVIN. Well then, show the money in court!

IAN. You're damn right I'll show it! But why do you
hand it over to me so freely if you committed murder
for the sake of it?

MELVIN. (*Contemplative, sitting down on the edge of
the bed.*) I don't need it anymore. I did have the idea
of beginning a new life with it, but I've lost interest.
I'll do other things. (*Lifting his water glass as if
making a toast.*) As you say, "Without God all
things are lawful." (*Taking a gulp or two.*)

IAN. I suppose now you believe in God!

MELVIN. No more than you do.

IAN. You are a fool!

> (MELVIN *crawls back into bed.* IAN
> *holds up the money.*)

Tomorrow I will show this in court. (*Slipping the bills into his pocket.*)

MELVIN. They'll merely say you've brought your own money!

> (IAN *angrily grabs* MELVIN *by his pajama top and violently shoves him against the pillows, leaning over him, both hands on his chest, one knee on the bed.*)

IAN. The only reason I don't kill you now is that I need you to testify in court tomorrow.

MELVIN. (*Eyes closed.*) Go ahead and kill me! You'd be doing both of us a favor.

IAN. (*Releasing* MELVIN, *then standing.*) I'll see you in court tomorrow. Tomorrow! (*Starting to go.*)

MELVIN. (*Quickly sitting up in bed.*) Ian! Wait! Show me the money again!

> (IAN *produces the money and thrusts it in* MELVIN*'s face.* MELVIN *stares at it for a full ten seconds.*)

Well, you can go now.

> (IAN *pockets the money and turns to go.*)

Ian!

IAN. (*Turning, impatient.*) What? Now what do you want?

> (MELVIN *grabs* IAN*'s forearm, then presses the back of* IAN*'s hand against*

MELVIN's cheek, holding it there momentarily, eyes closed.)

MELVIN. (*Softly.*) Adieu!

(IAN *pulls his hand away, walks to the door, then turns to* MELVIN.)

IAN. (*Emphatically.*) Tomorrow!

(*Fade-out.*)

SCENE 3

Ian's room, a little later. Ian's bed is more or less parallel to the footlights, but opposite in orientation to Melvin's bed in the previous scene. There is a stool at the foot of the bed. A book rests on the night table. IAN *enters and lies down on his bed. He attempts to read, gives up quickly, puts the book back on the night table, and holds his head in despair. After a few moments, the* VISITOR *appears out of nowhere. He resembles* IAN *except he is impish, even devilish, in speech and behavior.*

VISITOR. Excuse me for intruding. You've just been to see Melvin and learned some interesting things. Forgive me for telling you what you already know. That's one of my worst habits, one I can't seem to break.

(IAN *bolts up in bed, facing the* VISITOR, *who is now squatting on the stool at the foot of the bed, one hand on his chin.*)

IAN. Oh, God, I'm delirious! But I still have enough sense to know that it's really I myself who's speaking and not you. (*Tentatively.*) Right?

(VISITOR *grins broadly and chuckles faintly.*)

Well, talk to me about anything you like but not about religion! Make me laugh! Tell a joke or a funny story!

VISITOR. How charming!

IAN. Charming? Let's get one thing straight. Never for an instant do I assume that you're real. I know perfectly well who you are. You're a part of my illness. You're a hallucination!

VISITOR. You are so much more polite now than when we met the last time. (*Pause.*) I've been thinking about your decision.

IAN. What decision?

VISITOR. To defend your brother and, if necessary, sacrifice yourself for him. That's very noble.

IAN. (*Jumping out of bed.*) Shut up or I'll—

VISITOR. Yes?

IAN. Give you a swift kick!

VISITOR. A kick? How extraordinary! Well, go ahead and kick me! That would show you believe in me. You can't kick a hallucination.

IAN. I've never met anyone as irritating as you!

VISITOR. Sorry! See how I'm misunderstood! (*Pause.*) You want to know what I dream of most? Of becoming incarnate—taking the form of an ordinary man's wife and believing everything religion teaches. More than anything else in the world, I want to go to church and light a candle with simple faith. That would put an end to all my suffering. For that I'd gladly give up all my celebrity and life as a superstar.

IAN. You're a fool!

VISITOR. You keep calling me names. Have pity on someone less clever than you. Intelligence isn't everything. I have a kind and happy heart. That counts for something. Perhaps one day you'll see that. Do you know that last year (*Rubbing his lower back.*) I had a terrible attack of low back pain?

IAN. The Devil has back pain?

VISITOR. Why do you doubt it? If I take on flesh, I have to suffer the consequences. Nothing human is beyond me.

IAN. (*Chuckling.*) That's very good! You do have a sense of humor.

VISITOR. I'm glad I pleased you at last, even though I'm only a hallucination.

> (*The* VISITOR *slithers from the stool to the foot of the bed. Terrified,* IAN *vacates the bed and stands in amazement. The* VISITOR *continues insinuating himself to the head of the bed and makes himself comfortable, head on pillow, arms behind head, smiling.*)

IAN. Now you're really beginning to annoy me! Can't you just go away?

VISITOR. You expected something big of me, something extraordinary, but I've disappointed you. I'm sorry about that. (*Pause.*) Frankly, I simply yearn for annihilation. But no sooner do I say that than people who I thought didn't care at all about me say, "No! No! Live! Live! Life without you wouldn't be worth living! It would be an endless religious service— holy but tedious." And so I live because the people command me to.

IAN. (*Sitting on the stool at the foot of the bed.*) Does God exist?

VISITOR. (*Grinning.*) What can I say?

IAN. (*Angrily.*) Answer the question! Is there a God or isn't there?

VISITOR. My dear friend, I swear by all that's holy, I don't know.

IAN. (*Stunned.*) *You* don't know? Amazing!

VISITOR. (*Sitting up, grinning.*) Why is that amazing? Nothing in religion is certain. You must take religion —forgive me for saying so—on *faith*!

IAN. Well, at least tell me a funny story. You owe me that.

VISITOR. A funny story? I've already told you quite a few! I guess you didn't notice. Let's try this one: Once upon a time there lived here on earth a thinker. He rejected everything—God, faith, and above all the hereafter. One day he died. He was expecting oblivion, (*Standing.*) but instead he found a future life. He was astonished. And he was indignant. "This goes against my principles!" he shouted. (*Pause.*) You aren't laughing. You didn't think it was funny. You are angry, as usual. Forgive me. I'm only repeating a story I once heard.

IAN. You are a bad dream.

VISITOR. And yet, to judge by the passion with which you deny my existence, I am convinced you believe in me.

IAN. Nonsense! But strangely enough, I'd like to believe in you.

VISITOR. Just as I thought! You are longing for faith! You want to believe so much that you'd be willing to dine on locusts, wear filthy garments, and wander in the wilderness to save your soul!

IAN. (*Standing, angry.*) You scoundrel! I see what you're up to! You're working for the salvation of my soul!

VISITOR.   Why are you surprised?   Even *I* do good
works!   You see how I'm slandered!   But my, how
grouchy you are!

IAN.   I see your game!   You're tempting me the way you
tempt all holy men!

VISITOR.   (*Walking slowly to* IAN.)   Of course!   I
wouldn't deny it.   I do nothing else.   (*Grinning.*)   Oh,
something else!   I must admit I love to listen in at the
confessional!   What a delightful diversion!   However
depressed I may be beforehand, I'm always cheered up
afterward.   You have no idea what people tell priests
—or what priests do in the confessional.   You see, the
sex urge is a force to be reckoned with.   It is a force
mightier than belief in God.   Nature asserts her rights.
No amount of religion can interfere with nature.   One
day religion will learn that lesson—before it's too
late, I hope.

IAN.   (*Crawling into bed, curling up, and shutting his
eyes.*)   Go away and leave me alone!

VISITOR.   (*Standing at the head of the bed.*)   One last
thing, and I'll go.   Somebody takes credit for all
that's good in the world, but anything that's bad is
blamed on me!   Is that fair?   (*Shaking* IAN.)   Are you
asleep?

IAN.   No.   (*Pause.*)   I was thinking how to kill you.   (*He
sits up on the edge of his bed.*)

VISITOR.   Kill me?   Strong words.   If anyone kills me,
it'll be I myself.   (*Sitting down next to* IAN.)   I once
heard these words from a smart young man.   You
know the man I mean.

He said, "Actually, there's no need to destroy
anything except a man's belief that he alone has the
True Religion.   We must begin all reasonable
destruction with that.

(IAN *mouths the remaining words as the*
VISITOR *continues to speak them with-*
out interruption.)

Otherwise, one day it will destroy us all. Once people
learn to live with doubt—which alone permits
tolerance—they'll unite as brothers. And they'll share
in universal joy and happiness."

IAN. (*Getting out of bed, angrily.*) How dare *you* say
those words!

(IAN *picks up the book on the night*
table and hurls it at the VISITOR. *It*
flies over his head and across the room.)

VISITOR. How silly of you! You take me for a dream
and then hurl a book at me! Just like a woman!

(*Suddenly there is a loud persistent*
knocking on the door.   IAN *is be-*
wildered.)

You'd better open it! (*Grinning.*) It's your brother
Alex with surprising news.

(*The knocking continues, louder and*
more insistent.   IAN *moves toward the*
door with great difficulty and in slow
motion, as if straining every muscle to
break invisible chains. At last he seems
to break them, whereupon he suddenly
turns to face the room. The VISITOR
has vanished. IAN *stops and looks*
wildly about. He returns to the bed,
looks under it, yanks off the covers, and

*then stares at the empty stool. He turns
to the night table and finds the book he
recently hurled still there.   Puzzled, he
holds it up, examines it, and puts it back
on the table.   All the while the knocking
continues.*)

IAN. (*To the audience, in anguish.*) It was no dream! I
swear to you, it was no dream! It all happened just
as you saw! But I don't have to convince you.

> (*The knocking continues, more insistent.
> IAN goes to the door and opens it.*)

Alex! What are you doing here? What do you want?

ALEX. Melvin hanged himself!

> (*An instant of darkness serves as a
> visible exclamation point.*)

SCENE 4

*Ian's room. No time has passed. The lights immediately
come back on, and the play resumes where it left off.*

ALEX. Martha found him hanging just like he used to
hang one of his cats. He left a note that said, "I am
ending my life by my own free will so that I won't
have to testify against the killer." (*Concerned.*) Ian,
you don't look well!
IAN. I knew he'd hanged himself.
ALEX. How did you know?
IAN. *He* told me.

ALEX. *Who* told you?

IAN. *He* did. He was just here and suddenly slipped away. He saw you coming and was afraid. You are an angel, and he's afraid of angels.

ALEX. You're delirious!

IAN. What time is it?

ALEX. Nearly midnight.

IAN. It was no dream! (*Pointing to the stool.*) He was sitting right there!

ALEX. Who are you talking about?

IAN. The Devil. He's taken to visiting me. He visits me and he visits others. He says he even goes to bathhouses, which is pretty bold! When he's naked, you can be sure everyone can see his long tail!

ALEX. (*Concerned and comforting.*) Forget him!

IAN. He said to me, "You're going to confess that you murdered your father and that Douglas is innocent. And the only reason you're going to do that is to win the praise of men. You would do anything for that."

ALEX. Stop it! You didn't murder Dad!

IAN. He says that, too! He says I'm going to perform this act of nobility, and I don't even believe in nobility. And he says that's what's torturing me so! Well, he certainly knows what he's talking about!

ALEX. (*Alarmed.*) You're delirious!

IAN. Tomorrow I will take the stand and I'll tell who killed Father. But now that Melvin is dead, (*In anguish.*) who will believe me? And then (*Slowly scanning the room looking for someone.*) *he* will come and laugh at me.

(*Fade-out.*)

INTERMISSION

ACT III

SCENE 1

Courtroom, the next day. The Judge's bench is upstage center. On each side is a witness box. Perpendicular to the Judge's bench, on each side, are seats for the witnesses already seated: GREGORY, DR. HART, ALEX (no longer in clerical garb, wearing a suit), KATHRYN, THERESA, MARTHA, and IAN. In front of the Judge's bench is a small table with the material evidence: Karleton's bloodstained white robe, the fireplace poker, and the empty envelope with the name Theresa written on it. Downstage left sit the defendant, DOUG, and his lawyer, the DEFENDER. Downstage right sits the PROSECUTOR. The JUDGE enters and sits.

JUDGE. Douglas Karleton, please rise and tell the court how you plead to the charges of robbery and murder of your father.

DOUG. *(Rising.)* I plead guilty to drunkenness and dissipation, to idleness and debauchery, and I'm a scoundrel. But I'm not guilty of robbing and murdering my father. *(Sitting.)*

JUDGE. Douglas Karleton, you must answer only what is asked and not run off into irrelevant matters. I don't want to have to tell you this again.

DOUG. Your Honor, I'm sorry. I won't, I promise. It just blurted out. I won't do it again.

JUDGE. The trial may proceed. First witness. Gregory. Please take the stand.

GREGORY. My name is Gregory. I was the deceased Mr. Karleton's caretaker, gardener, and maintenance man. I lived in the servants' part of the house for more

75

than twenty years with my wife and also the recently deceased cook, Melvin.

PROSECUTOR. (*Standing and walking toward* GREGORY.) Tell the court what happened the night of the murder.

GREGORY. I heard noises in the garden, a loud rustling of bushes. I quickly went out the back door to the garden. I saw Doug there. I was surprised to see him because I was expecting to find a thief. When he saw me, he jumped over the garden wall and ran off. I'm certain that he had come from Karleton's bedroom because the door from Karleton's bedroom to the garden was wide open.

PROSECUTOR. You didn't leave the house by the open bedroom door?

GREGORY. No, that was Karleton's private door from his bedroom. I left by the back door near the servants' quarters.

PROSECUTOR. Tell the court something of the relationship between Karleton and his son Douglas.

GREGORY. It was not cordial.

PROSECUTOR. Can you be more specific?

GREGORY. They argued a lot.

PROSECUTOR. What did they argue about?

GREGORY. Two things mainly, money and women. Doug was unhappy that he had not received his full inheritance from his mother. Karleton kept most of it, including the house in which he lived and the woods and the farm upstate, and said that Doug had received all he was going to get.

PROSECUTOR. And what did they argue about concerning women?

GREGORY. They argued mostly about one woman— Theresa. They both were in love with her. Doug wanted to marry her, and Karleton—

PROSECUTOR. Yes? Continue.

GREGORY. Karleton wanted to sleep with her.

PROSECUTOR.   Did Doug ever threaten to kill his father?

GREGORY. Oh yes! He said that if Karleton ever slept with Theresa, he'd kill him.   And to make his point, Doug once grabbed Karleton and threw him to the floor.

PROSECUTOR. Did Doug strike his father often?

GREGORY. No, that was the only time I ever saw it; and I never heard anyone talk about such things.

PROSECUTOR. Was Karleton a good father?

GREGORY. No, he wasn't a good father to Doug or to any of his sons.   He had no interest in them when they were children.   He never played with them and had no part in their upbringing. Once when Doug was a little boy, his head was covered with lice. Karleton was disgusted at the sight and threw the child out of the house. The crying boy came running to me. I spent hours combing his hair and cleaning him up.

PROSECUTOR.   Karleton had three legitimate sons by two wives. Is that right?

GREGORY. Yes.

PROSECUTOR. His first wife—Doug's mother—was very wealthy. His second wife—Ian and Alex's mother—was a poor woman who was very religious. Is that right?

GREGORY. Yes. Douglas's mother died before I came to the house. Karleton immediately remarried; and his new wife hired me. She was a fine woman, extraordinarily beautiful and highly religious.   She was the mother of Ian and Alex. Karleton ridiculed her on matters of religion—and at the same time, he was sleeping with other women, often in his own home, even holding orgies there in his wife's presence!   One day she ran off—some say with a divinity student—and never returned.

PROSECUTOR. Tell us a little about Melvin.

GREGORY. Melvin was Karleton's illegitimate son. His mother was a poor homeless creature who died giving birth to him in Karleton's garden. My wife and I were childless, and we asked Karleton whether we could raise the infant. He seemed happy at the idea.

PROSECUTOR. Was Melvin reliable? Honest?

GREGORY. Oh yes! Karleton trusted him completely, and rightly so. He never stole a thing and never would.

PROSECUTOR. On the night of the murder, you say the door from Karleton's bedroom to the garden was wide open?

GREGORY. When I ran into the garden and found Doug there, I could see the door wide open.

PROSECUTOR. I have no more questions. (*Sits.*)

DEFENDER. (*Stands.*) Gregory, you saw Doug in the garden, and you saw the open door. You think Doug ran out of the house by that door, but you are not sure, are you?

GREGORY. How else could he get into the garden?

DEFENDER. You reported that Doug left the garden by jumping over the garden wall. Couldn't he have entered the garden the same way? And perhaps he wasn't in the house at all. Isn't that so?

GREGORY. That's possible, but I don't think that's what happened.

DEFENDER. Couldn't Karleton himself have gone into the garden?

GREGORY. No, he kept that door locked and never went into the garden at night.

DEFENDER. Was the main door to the house also kept locked at night?

GREGORY. Yes.

DEFENDER. Well, how could Doug gain access to the house? Did he have a key?

GREGORY. No, he had no key. And after the incident when he threw Karleton to the floor, we had strict orders never to admit him to the house again.

DEFENDER. The police investigators reported no signs of forced entry. So whoever came into the bedroom had to have been let in by Karleton. And you say that Karleton would never admit Doug. That, to my way of thinking, would exclude Doug as the murderer.

GREGORY. You have your way of thinking, and I have mine!

DEFENDER. Were you in bed when you heard Doug in the garden?

GREGORY. No, I was in the dining room.

DEFENDER. What were you doing there?

GREGORY. I was—drinking.

DEFENDER. Drinking what?

GREGORY. Whiskey.

DEFENDER. How much whiskey had you drunk when you heard Doug? One shot? Two?

GREGORY. Oh, more than that!

DEFENDER. A wine glass? Two?

GREGORY. More than that!

DEFENDER. How much more?

GREGORY. About two or three tumblers full—neat!

DEFENDER. When you went into the garden, were you sober?

GREGORY. No, I wouldn't say that. I was rather— high.

DEFENDER. Did you run into the garden or walk?

GREGORY. To tell the truth, I staggered.

DEFENDER. You staggered, and you saw Doug?

GREGORY. Yes.

DEFENDER. And you saw the bedroom door wide open?

GREGORY. That's right!

DEFENDER. In your state, I dare say, you might well have seen the gates of heaven wide open!

PROSECUTOR. (*Jumping up.*) I object!
JUDGE. What are you objecting to?

(*The* PROSECUTOR *sits.*)

DEFENDER. Gregory, do you know whether you were
    awake when you saw the open door?
GREGORY. Well, I know I was standing on both my
    legs.
DEFENDER. That's no proof you were awake.
GREGORY. I was awake. I'm sure of it! Because then I
    began to sing, and I lay down on the ground to make
    myself more comfortable. But still I was awake,
    because I knew I was singing.
DEFENDER. If someone had asked you the day of the
    week, could you have answered the question?
GREGORY. Of course!
DEFENDER. What was the day of the week?
GREGORY. Mmm. I'm not sure.
DEFENDER. What day is today?
GREGORY. Today is—
DEFENDER. Yes?
GREGORY. Today is—I'm not sure. But I am sure the
    door was open.
DEFENDER. I have no more questions.
DOUG. (*Standing and shouting.*) Except for the door,
    everything this dear old man said is true. As for
    combing the lice off me when I was a child, that is
    true. And I thank him for it. And I remember loving
    him for it at the time, and I love him still. But about
    the door, he is mistaken!
JUDGE.   Will the defendant sit down and be quiet!
    I don't want to have to tell you that again!

*   *   *   *   *   *

(*Asterisks, here and subsequently, indicate that the lights quickly fade out and then quickly fade in, each time with the old witness gone from one box, and the new witness already in place in the opposite box.*)

PROSECUTOR.   Dr. Hart, you are well-known in this town and well-thought-of. You have been called as a medical witness to comment on the defendant's health, particularly his mental health. You are called not as an expert in psychiatry, which you are not, but as an expert in family medicine, which you are, and also as an impartial observer of the defendant's behavior in the community.   Doctor, would you describe the defendant as mentally ill?

DR. HART.   (*Trace of a German accent.*)   I would not call him mentally ill. But I would not say that he is normal either. Anyone can see that. His inability to restrain himself in the courtroom from outbursts is characteristic of him. He simply has to say whatever is on his mind the moment it occurs to him. That is not necessarily a sign of mental illness. It is, rather, a sign of immaturity, like a child's behavior, like a young boy who simply cannot wait to tell the teacher the answer to a question or who cannot wait to share his observations.

Such children when they become adults and continue to exhibit this behavior can be irritating to others, but they are not necessarily ill. In many ways, Doug is still like a young boy. That is part of his downfall and also part of his charm. It is one of the features, if I may say so, that make him so attractive to women and so unpopular with men.

PROSECUTOR.   Could his illness have caused him to commit murder?

DR. HART.   (*Sharply.*)   First of all, I have not said that he has an illness. Second, it has not been established that he has committed a murder. That is the purpose of this trial, if I understand the purpose of this trial. (*Pause.*)

I do not wish to sound impertinent, but I have been summoned here to describe his personality from the point of view of a family doctor, and I shall try to confine my remarks to the job that I have been assigned to do. *Hmm?* [*A crisp German sound meaning, "Is that clear?"*] (*Pause.*)

In my opinion, the defendant is an impetuous young man with a highly intelligent and very quick mind—much more impatient than impulsive. I am unwilling to say that he would do something criminal just because of his impatient personality. Expressing one's thoughts and feelings and committing criminal acts are entirely different matters.

PROSECUTOR. Are you saying, then, that he could *not* have committed the murder?

DR. HART. (*Irritated.*) No, I am not saying that! Given the right set of circumstances, anyone in this courtroom is capable of committing murder!

PROSECUTOR. Please tell us more, Doctor, about the defendant's personality as you know him.

DR. HART. I first knew him as a child. (*Looking at* DOUG *fondly, smiling.*) He had a good heart as a child. And I know him now as an adult. And he still has a good heart. I am confident that had his early life been different, things would have turned out differently for him. There is an old proverb: "If a man has one head, that is good. But if another head comes along to help, it would be better still, because then he would have two heads."

PROSECUTOR. Forgive me, Doctor, but the proverb is "Two heads are better than one."

DR. HART. Exactly! Thank you!

PROSECUTOR. Now that we have the proverb, what does it have to do with the defendant?

DR. HART. Why, everything! Don't you see? Douglas
had a good head. But in his childhood he did not
meet another head to guide him, so his good
judgment went away. Without guidance from an adult
male, his judgment wandered aimlessly until it fell
into a pit so deep he could not get out. And no one
came along to help him. And that is why he is here
today, and that is why we are all here today. (*Pause.*)

But I remember him as a child. What a wonderful
boy! So grateful and appreciative—and neglected!
Neglected by his own father. I saw the little boy
running about alone in the backyard; and although his
father was at home, he never played with him.

I was a new doctor in town then and a young man.
I came from Germany. (*Defensively.*) You notice my
accent? (*Continuing his narration.*) And I would see
this child when I passed his house as I walked to my
office. He was friendly and kind. Sometimes I would
stop and play catch with him. How sad, I thought,
for a rich boy to be so neglected. I wanted to give
this child a gift. What would please a boy like this?
And then I thought of the very thing, something all
little boys like. So I decided to buy him a bag of—a
bag of—what is the word? Surely you know what I
mean?

PROSECUTOR. (*Tentatively.*) Apples?

DR. HART. (*Annoyed.*) No! Not apples! Apples grow
on trees! These grow underground. They are small.
You crack the shells with your fingers, and if you
can't do it with your fingers, you put them in your
mouth and crack them with your teeth.

PROSECUTOR. (*Tentatively.*) Peanuts?

DR. HART. (*Relieved.*) Yes! Peanuts! I bought him a
bag of peanuts, and I gave it to him. I have never
seen a happier expression on a child's face in all my
life! And after he had eaten some, I lifted my index

finger and said, "Now I am going to teach you a line from one of the most beautiful and joyous songs in all the world." (*Singing the following line from Beethoven's* "Ode to Joy.")

Alle Menschen werden Brüder,
Wo dein sanfter Flügel weilt.

PROSECUTOR. What does that mean, Doctor?

DR. HART.   It means, "All men become brothers wherever Joy comes and lands on her gentle wings." He quickly learned this, and then I went to the office. Two days later I happened to be passing his house again, and he came running up to me very excited and said, "Uncle! Listen!" And he sang in tune and in perfect German, "*Alle Menschen werden Brüder, Wo dein sanfter Flügel weilt.*" (*Pause.*)

Days passed, and I did not see him again. They said he had been shipped off to boarding school. (*Pause.*)

Over twenty years pass. I am sitting one morning in my study when my wife brings into the room a magnificent-looking young army officer whom I would never have recognized except that he held up his index finger and sang, "*Alle Menschen werden Brüder, Wo dein sanfter Flügel weilt.*" I jumped from my chair and hugged him, I was so overjoyed to see him. "What brings you here?" I asked.   He responded, "I have just returned from active duty, and I have come to thank you for the bag of peanuts. No one else ever gave me a true gift. Only you." And he hugged me.

I had totally forgotten the incident, but it came back to me in an instant. And I suddenly remembered that poor child in the yard, and my heart was touched to the breaking point. And we shed tears, and we laughed. And now! Oh, *mein Gott*! (*Weeping.*)

DOUG. (*Standing and shouting.*) Oh, good doctor! Oh, good man!

> (*The* JUDGE *does not intervene.   He does not even move.*)

*   *   *   *   *   *

ALEX. My name is Alex Karleton. I am the youngest brother of the defendant.

PROSECUTOR.   Did your brother ever tell you he intended to kill your father?

ALEX. He never used words like that.

PROSECUTOR. What words did he use?

ALEX. He once told me of his hatred for him and of his fear that in an unguarded moment of intense rage, he might be capable of murdering him.

PROSECUTOR. Did you believe him?

ALEX. No, because I never doubted that some higher feeling would always intervene and save him from his baser feelings, as, indeed, is the case. Doug did not kill our father. Melvin did.

*   *   *   *   *   *

KATHRYN.   My name is Kathryn. I'm a friend of Douglas Karleton's.

PROSECUTOR. A *friend*? Is that all?

KATHRYN. I was once engaged to him, but he broke the engagement.

PROSECUTOR.   How did it happen that you lent five thousand to a man who broke the engagement?

KATHRYN. At the moment I lent it, I didn't know the engagement was broken. But I would have lent it anyway. In fact, I did not lend it at all. I gave it to him. It was an outright gift. He once had been very kind to me, lending me a huge sum of money to spare my family financial embarrassment. It was a highly noble act because he hardly knew me at the time, and still he lent me a small fortune without hesitation. I'd rather not talk about this, since it has no bearing on the case.

PROSECUTOR.   Please explain why the five thousand represented a gift from you and not a loan.

KATHRYN. It was not so much a gift from me as from my father. When he died, I returned to Doug the fortune he had lent my father and gave him an additional five thousand as a gift, which I was certain my father would have wanted him to have.

PROSECUTOR. Doug admits to having squandered the twenty-five thousand. What happened to your gift?

KATHRYN. I really don't know. You'll have to ask him.

PROSECUTOR. Did Doug ever tell you he intended to murder his father?

KATHRYN. (*Reflecting.*) No.

*   *   *   *   *   *

THERESA. My name is Theresa.

PROSECUTOR. What was your relationship to the murdered man?

THERESA. We had no relationship! Anything you may have heard is nonsense! Was it my fault he was attracted to me and harassed me? I saw him once or twice, but nothing happened except he couldn't take his eyes off me.

But it's true—I led him on. I shouldn't have done that. I never had any interest in him, and at the time I wasn't even sure I was in love with Doug. But I must admit that it did please me to have both a father and a son in love with me, fighting over me. That's why the murder was committed. I've brought them to this! It's my fault! All my fault!

PROSECUTOR. Did you ever see the envelope with money for you?

THERESA. No, but I heard about it from that evil monster! I only laughed. I wouldn't have slept with Karleton for all the money in the world! And the nerve of him, thinking he could win me over with money!

PROSECUTOR. You spoke of "that evil monster." Whom did you mean?

THERESA. Melvin! Who else? The one who murdered Karleton and hanged himself last night! (*Suddenly pointing to* KATHRYN.)   Kathryn—sitting over there!— She is the cause of all this! She loved Doug and loves him still! She's the cause of all this.

PROSECUTOR. But when you first took the stand, you said that you were the cause of all this.

THERESA. Oh, I don't know what I mean! Everyone was saying Doug killed his father; and if that was true, then it would be all my fault. But when he told me he wasn't guilty, I believed him immediately. And I believe him still and always will.

*   *   *   *   *   *

MARTHA. My name is Martha. I am Gregory's wife and Karleton's housekeeper.

PROSECUTOR. Where were you the night of the murder?

MARTHA. Sleeping in my bed.

PROSECUTOR. Was your husband beside you?

MARTHA. He was, through most of the night. Then he got up because he couldn't sleep. I couldn't sleep either, but I stayed in bed.

PROSECUTOR. Why couldn't you sleep?

MARTHA.   Because Melvin, who sleeps in the next room, was snoring so loudly!

PROSECUTOR. Did you ever fall asleep that night?

MARTHA. No, but it was not only the snoring that kept me awake. I was also worried.

PROSECUTOR. What were you worried about?

MARTHA. Ian was away, which left the house defenseless. I was afraid something might happen.

PROSECUTOR. What were you afraid of?

MARTHA. With Ian away, I was afraid Douglas might harm Karleton.

PROSECUTOR. So you didn't sleep at all that night?

MARTHA. Not a wink. And when I heard the commotion in the garden, I went out there to see what was going on.

PROSECUTOR. And what *was* going on?

MARTHA. Gregory was lying drunk and shouting that Doug had killed Karleton. He told me to call the police. So I ran back into the house and called the police.

PROSECUTOR. Did you see Doug that night? Did you notice whether the bedroom door to the garden was open?

MARTHA. No. I didn't see Doug, and I didn't notice the bedroom door.

*   *   *   *   *   *

IAN. My name is Ian Karleton.

JUDGE. Ian Karleton, you look ill. Are you too ill to testify? If you are ill, you need not.

IAN. I appreciate the concern of the court, but I'm well enough to testify. And I can tell you interesting things.

PROSECUTOR. Did you ever hear your brother Doug threaten to murder your father?

IAN. Yes, once. And I heard about the money in the envelope, too. That I heard from Melvin. (*Pause.*) Your Honor, I suddenly feel very ill and wish to be excused. (*Long pause.*) No, it's passed. I feel better. I can continue. I'm like the country girl. You see, they were putting on her wedding gown to take her to church to be married, and she said, "I'll go if I like, and I won't if I don't." It's from a poem.

JUDGE. What do you mean by it?

IAN. (*Pulling out the bills in a money clip.*) Why, simply this! (*Holding up the money.*) These are the bills that were in the envelope. This is the very money over which my father was murdered. Where shall I put it?

> (*The* GUARD *takes the money and hands it to the* JUDGE, *who puts it next to his gavel, where it remains.*)

JUDGE. How did this money come into your possession?

IAN. I got it from Melvin last night.

> (*A stir in the courtroom.*)

PROSECUTOR. Did he tell you where he got it?

IAN. Yes. He said he stole it from Father.

> (*Another stir.*)

PROSECUTOR. When did he steal it?

IAN. The night of the murder. (*Pause.*) Melvin went into Father's bedroom. They argued. Father called him names—vile, insulting, insinuating names. Melvin got angry and killed him. Then he took the five thousand from its hiding place and tossed the envelope on the floor to cast guilt on Doug, whom

everyone would expect to do such a careless thing.
Melvin then returned to his room and went to bed.

PROSECUTOR. How did you learn those things?

IAN. From Melvin. He told them to me last night. He
told me everything. And then he gave me the money
just before he hanged himself. It was he, not Doug,
who killed our father. Melvin told me so.

PROSECUTOR. Why did Melvin steal the money?

IAN. He was planning to open a restaurant. He needed
money to do that. He expected nothing from my
father.

PROSECUTOR. Well, if he stole the money to open a
restaurant, why did he give the money to you?

IAN. He changed his mind. He decided to kill himself
instead.

PROSECUTOR. How do you know that?

IAN. What other explanation makes sense? And if that
story doesn't make sense, let me tell you one that
does.

PROSECUTOR. Yes?

IAN. Melvin did *not* kill my father.

(*A stir.*)

PROSECUTOR. Ian, first you said Melvin killed your
father, but now you say he did not kill your father.
Did he kill your father or not?

IAN. He did not.

PROSECUTOR. Do you know who *did* kill your father?

IAN. Yes, I do.

PROSECUTOR. Well, then, tell us! Who did kill your
father?

IAN. I did.

(*A loud stir and gasping.*)

I killed him, but Melvin was my instrument. It's like
when God led the children of Israel out of Egypt but
Moses was his instrument. Or it's like when the
heavenly Father so loved the world that he sent his
son as a sacrificial victim to take away the sins of the
world, but some Jews and Romans were his
instrument.

PROSECUTOR. You mean that Melvin killed your father
at your command?

IAN. No. He knew I wanted my father dead, so he killed
him for me, out of love for me. (*Pause.*) Oh, I know
you think I'm lying or out of my mind, but I'm not
lying and not out of my mind. I can produce a
witness who will verify everything I've said.

PROSECUTOR. Who is this witness?

IAN. (*Pause*) My witness has a long tail. He comes and
talks to me at night.

PROSECUTOR. Are you in your right mind?

IAN. I think I'm in my right mind. I'm in the same evil
mind as all of you, in the same mind as all these ugly
faces. (*Pointing to the audience.*) My father has been
murdered, and they're all horrified. Hypocrites! They
want a spectacle! They want a show! Bread and
circuses! Why else did they come? (*To the* JUDGE.)
Your Honor, have you any water? (*Pause.*) Give me
a glass of water, for Christ's sake!

ALEX. (*Jumping up, shouting.*) Your Honor, he is ill!
He cannot be believed!

> (*A loud stir throughout the courtroom.
> Comments are heard, such as "He's out
> of it," "He's lost it," "He's mentally
> ill," "He doesn't belong on the stand."*)

JUDGE. (*Pounding the gavel.*) Order! Order!

(*The courtroom becomes quiet.*)

IAN. Don't be upset! I'm only a murderer! But I'm not crazy! And I'm not delirious! But you want proof, and that's the problem. I have no proof because Melvin refuses to send you proof from the grave. And there are no other witnesses.

PROSECUTOR. But you said you had a witness.

IAN. Oh yes! One, perhaps. Yes, I have one!

JUDGE. Where is your witness?

IAN. (*Looking around.*) He's here somewhere! The Devil has to be in a court of law somewhere! How stupid this business all is. Come, Your Honor, take me, not Doug. Why, oh why, is everyone so stupid! (*Pause.*) Oh, how I would give anything for one moment of joy!

> (*The* JUDGE *nods to the* GUARD, *who then approaches* IAN.)

> (*To the* GUARD.) What the hell do you think you're doing!

> (*The* GUARD *takes* IAN *by the arms and proceeds to remove him as he struggles, babbles, and yells incoherently. The court is in pandemonium. The* JUDGE *pounds his gavel without success.* KATHRYN *approaches the bench and says something privately to the* JUDGE.)

JUDGE. (*Pounding the gavel and restoring order.*) Kathryn will take the stand again.

KATHRYN. I want to make sure I did not perjure myself the first time. The prosecutor asked me whether

Douglas had ever talked of murdering his father, and I
said no. Let me say, I discarded the idea as altogether
incredible, and I still consider it incredible; but in
fact, Doug did come to see me once and said, "I may
be forced to rob my father as soon as Ian leaves the
house, and that might lead to murder." And that is
exactly what happened! Poor, dear Ian! He's been
going out of his mind trying to save his brother. But
I could not stand by and let him do that. I had to tell
the truth!

THERESA. (*Standing up, shouting.*) First you lie to
protect Douglas! Now you lie to protect Ian! Your
lies will end up destroying us all!

> (*A stir while the* JUDGE *pounds the
> gavel.*)

> (*Fade-out.*)

SCENE 2

Courtroom, a little later.

JUDGE. The Prosecutor will deliver his summation.

> (*As the* PROSECUTOR *now [and the*
> DEFENDER *later] gives his summation,
> he mostly paces slowly back and forth
> downstage, frequently facing the
> audience, which represents the jury.*)

PROSECUTOR. Ladies and gentlemen of the jury, we
have here the case of a murdered father whose only
purpose in life was the gratification of his sensual

pleasure. He abandoned his small and motherless
children to servants and boarding schools and was
glad to be rid of them. His self-indulgence knew no
bounds. His motto was "The world can go to hell so
long as things go well for me." Everyone agrees he
was an inadequate father. But that is not grounds for
murder; otherwise, there would be many murdered
fathers. But enough about the father. Let us turn to
the defendant, to the son. (*Pause.*)

Douglas is a lover of Beethoven and Schiller, and
yet he haunts our local taverns. Oh, he can be good,
but give him the wild life! For this he needs money,
a great deal of it! Moreover, he desperately needed
five thousand to pay off his former fiancée, Kathryn,
to be rid of her and begin a new life with Theresa—
who happened to be the love of his own father and for
whom his father had set aside five thousand. And to
pay off his former fiancée, the defendant swore he
would kill his father to get the five thousand.
(*Pause.*)

Some suspicion has been cast on Melvin, but
Melvin is not on trial. To suspect Melvin is absurd.
And now Melvin is dead. How convenient to accuse a
dead man! If Melvin had killed Karleton, why did he
not leave a suicide note saying, "I am killing myself
because I killed my father and cannot bear to live with
my guilt." He did not say that because he did not do
that. (*Pause.*)

Ian produced five thousand. Where did Ian get it?
We will never know, but we must not believe he got
it from Melvin! Why should we? Ian is sick and
delirious and making a desperate effort to save his
brother by blaming a dead man.

Let us abandon preposterous ideas and focus on
what really happened. Douglas went into the
bedroom. He picked up the poker (*Picking up the*

poker and pantomiming.) and killed his father. He saw the envelope with the money (*Returning the poker to the table, picking up the envelope, pretending to remove the contents, and dropping the envelope on the floor.*), took the money, dropped the envelope on the floor, and ran out Karleton's bedroom door to the garden. (*Picking up the envelope from the floor and returning it to the table.*)

Ladies and gentlemen of the jury, let us deal only with facts. (*Holding up and showing the blood-stained robe, then putting it back on the table.*) A father has been brutally murdered by his son. Do not heap the world's scorn on this court by a verdict justifying the murder of the father by the son! (*He glowers at* DOUG, *then sits.*)

JUDGE. The defense will deliver its summation.

DEFENDER. Ladies and gentlemen of the jury, the prosecution maintains that because Doug was in Karleton's garden and because an inebriated caretaker saw an open bedroom door, Douglas had to have been in Karleton's bedroom. The prosecution also maintains that because an empty envelope was found on the bedroom floor, Douglas must have stolen the money that was presumably in the envelope. The prosecution, having concluded that Douglas was in the bedroom and robbed Karleton, maintains that Douglas must have killed him! What kind of reasoning is this? It is a fantastic chain made from unconnected links! (*Pause.*)

Now, I must ask, who did kill Karleton? (*Pause.*) Melvin. Melvin has been accused by four people. This cannot be dismissed. (*Pause.*) Ian produced five thousand—the judge, the prosecutor, and I counted it during the recess, and there was indeed five thousand. Ian says Melvin told him it was the same five thousand he stole from Karleton after he had murdered him. But the prosecution throws out this testimony because Ian is delirious. (*Pause.*)

And the prosecution asks, if Melvin killed Karleton, why did he not confess his guilt in his suicide note? To answer this question, we must discriminate between guilt and despair. They are different emotions and evoke different forms of behavior. Guilt evokes atonement, the capability to say, "I am sorry. Forgive me." But despair does the opposite. Despair is not sorry. It does not ask forgiveness. Despair is vindictive and may evoke the most malignant form of vengeance. There is nothing a desperate man will not do—from killing himself to killing everyone around him, from setting fire to a house to setting fire, if it were possible, to the entire world. In taking his own life, the despairing suicide inflicts on himself the uncontrollable rage he feels against all those whom he has envied or hated all his life. (*Pause.*)

The problem with the theories invented by the prosecution is that not a single one is supported by evidence. Are we to destroy a man by imaginary theories? If this was an ordinary case of murder, the case would be dismissed. What makes this case extraordinary is that it is one in which a son allegedly murdered his father. That impresses people; and the lack of evidence suddenly doesn't matter, not even to fair and unprejudiced minds. (*Pause.*)

My client as a child was left to the care of Providence like a beast in the field. And still, by all the testimony, when he grew up, he had a kind and generous disposition. Moreover, for all his reported debauchery, he is not without a serious sense of responsibility. He became, after all, an army officer and served this nation faithfully, and recently received an honorable discharge. Members of the jury, because

there is not a shred of evidence against him, you must
find Douglas Karleton not guilty of murdering and
robbing his father.   You must show the world that
there are good people watching over our nation's
system of justice. (*Sits.*)

(*Fade-out.*)

SCENE 3

Courtroom, later.

JUDGE.   Ladies and gentlemen of the jury, have you
　　reached a verdict?

FOREMAN. (*Rising.*) We have, Your Honor.

JUDGE. Is the defendant, Douglas Karleton, guilty or not
　　guilty of the charge of robbery of his father?

FOREMAN. We the jury find the defendant, Douglas
　　Karleton (*Pause.*) guilty of the robbery of his father.

JUDGE. Is the defendant guilty or not guilty of the charge
　　of murder of his father?

FOREMAN.   We find the defendant (*Pause.*) guilty of the
　　murder of his father.

(*A loud stir.*)

JUDGE. (*Pounding the gavel.*)   Order!   We must have
　　order!

> (*There is shouting in the courtroom,
> with individuals exclaiming "What is
> the meaning of this?" "Outrageous!"
> "What next?" etc.*)

No more outbursts! Order! (*Pounding the gavel, restoring order.*)

DOUG. (*Standing, weeping, hands outstretched.*) I swear by Almighty God, I did not murder and rob my father! So I can't be convicted of that! No. I'm being punished for my war crimes! I'm being punished for the baby with the blue fists and for all the other innocent children I murdered in combat! So I accept the judgment of the court. I'm no longer afraid to die. (*Sitting, still sobbing.*)

JUDGE. Douglas Karleton, please rise for sentencing.

(DOUG *rises, calm.*)

Douglas Karleton, this court sentences you for the murder and robbery of your father to life imprisonment.

(*Scattered gasps in the courtroom.*)

(*Pounding the gavel.*) Court is dismissed.

(*Fade-out.*)

SCENE 4

Cemetery, a few weeks later. In various stages of mourning standing around a grave are ALEX, DOUG *in prison garb and handcuffed to a* GUARD *at his side,* THERESA *at the* GUARD*'s other side,* KATHRYN, *who carries a rose,* DR. HART, MARTHA, *and* GREGORY. *After a moment,* KATHRYN *stoops, places the rose on the grave, then stands.* ALEX *embraces her comfortingly. Then* ALEX *steps forward and speaks.*

ALEX.   We are gathered here to bury the ashes of my brother Ian. Ian did not want a religious service, and he did not want eulogies. Nonetheless, I should like to say a few words in his honor and memory, words written by Ian himself many years ago. (*Removing a small book from his jacket pocket, opening it to a marked place, and reading.*)

> Actually, there is no need to destroy anything except the belief that there is one *True* Religion, for the sake of which men hate one another and are willing to slay one another. Once we rid ourselves of that notion and learn to live with uncertainty,
>
> (*The music of the hymn based on Beethoven's "Ode to Joy" begins softly and swells gently to the end of the speech.*)
>
> all men can unite as brothers and can share in universal joy and happiness. And eternal peace shall come to the earth at last.

(*Fade-out.*)

THE END

(*During the curtain call, it is effective to play a recording of Beethoven's Symphony #9, 4th movement, beginning at* "Freude" *and continuing to* "Alle Menschen werden Brüder, Wo dein sanfter Flügel weilt."*—Bars 542–594, segue 928–940.*)

THE PLAYWRIGHT

Howard Rubenstein is a physician and a playwright. He was born in 1931 in Chicago and received a B.A. from Carleton College in 1953 and an M.D. from Harvard Medical School in 1957. In 1967 he was appointed Physician and Chief of Allergy at the Harvard University Health Services, a position he held until 1989, when he became a medical consultant to the Department of Social Services, State of California, a position he held until 2000, the year he retired from the practice of medicine.

Rubenstein translated Aeschylus' *Agamemnon*, which was produced at Granite Hills Acting Workshop (GHAW), El Cajon, California, in 1997. A videotape of a performance of that production was requested by Oliver Taplin, Regius Professor, Oxford, and may be found in the Archive of Performances of Greek and Roman Drama, University of Oxford, England. Rubenstein then translated and adapted Euripides' *The Trojan Women*, produced at GHAW in 2001. That production was the most decorated show, professional and amateur, of the 2001 San Diego theater season (*San Diego Playbill*).

Rubenstein has also written an epic in free verse titled *Maccabee*.

Howard Rubenstein and his wife, Judy, have four grown children.